Sing it !

LEARN ENGLISH THROUGH SONG

Text/Workbook
Level Three

Millie Grenough

Technical Review:
Manuel C.R. Dos Santos
ELT Consultant/Author

McGRAW-HILL

México, Santafé de Bogotá, Buenos Aires, Caracas, Guatemala, Lisbon, Madrid, New York, Panamá, São Paulo,

Auckland, Hamburg, London, Milan, Montreal, New Delhi, Paris, San Francisco, St. Louis, Sydney, Singapore, Tokyo, Toronto

Design: Jorge Martínez and M. E. Aslett, Inc.

Developmental Editor/ELT Publisher: Louise Jennewine

Music Engraving: Tony Finno, Joe Muccioli and the King Brand Company

Permissions Coordinator: Lowell Britson

Publishing Coordinator: Janet Gomolson

SING IT! LEARN ENGLISH THROUGH SONG, Level Three

ISBN: 0-07-024709-9 Text/Workbook, Level Three
       0-07-024711-0 Cassette, Level Three
       0-07-911682-5 Set, Level Three

1234567890   P.E.94   9012356784

Impreso en México   Printed in Mexico

Esta obra se terminó de
imprimir en septiembre de 1994
en Programas Educativos, S.A. de C.V.
Calz. Chabacano Núm. 65-A
Col. Asturias
Deleg. Cuauhtémoc
06850 México, D.F.

Se tiraron 7,700 ejemplares

SING IT!
LEARN ENGLISH
THROUGH SONG

*is dedicated to the spirit of song
in all of us.*

ABOUT THE AUTHOR

MILLIE GRENOUGH grew up in a singing family in Kentucky, learned Spanish from people and songs in Bolivia, Colombia, Mexico, Nicaragua, Panama, Peru, Puerto Rico and Spain, and has taught English as a Foreign and Second Language to people from more than twenty countries. Millie is also a Clinical Social Worker and a professional singer. She is co-producer of the cassette "MOSAIC: New Haven Sings of Peace and War" and has developed teaching curricula for Headstart, Adult Basic Education Programs, the Instituto de Estudios Norteamericanos in Barcelona and the International Relations Center at Yale University.

CONTENTS

Key Structures	**Review:** Present and Future Tenses, Imperative, Contractions, Prepositions, "There"
	Verb + "er" = Noun: I'm a dreamer
Communicative Objectives	To talk about imagination
	To plan your own dreams for the world and discuss them

Key Structures	**Comparisons:** "As"+ Adjective + "As," "like"+ Noun
	Non-standard English
	Review: Present and Present Continuous Tenses, Reductions
Communicative Objectives	To make comparisons
	To discuss city and country living
	To give reasons for your preferences

Key Structures	**Phrasal Verbs:** arms reach out, road leads back
	Noun + "ful" = Adjective: in peaceful dreams I see
	Review: Present Tense, "As" + Adjective + "As"
Communicative Objectives	To talk about home and about being "homesick"
	To describe various people and places in detail

Why sing English?

Because music gets into our subconscious quickly and subtly, and because songs are a powerful medium for acquiring new knowledge and for reinforcing already-learned structures.

Throughout the world, English is probably encountered more often today in music than on the printed page. English students in Mexico City, Rio de Janeiro or Tokyo may hear little spoken English outside their English classes, but all of them are exposed to American and English songs on radio, TV, and in movies. Many of them are familiar with traditional folk and spiritual melodies and even sing these songs in their native languages. These people, as well as new arrivals in New York or London, readily tune in to songs. Once they are introduced to specific songs, they practice, consciously or unconsciously, for many hours outside class.

SING IT!, First Edition helped many people learn English. Since the response to the first edition was so positive, many of the songs and the structure that made SING IT! successful and fun to use have been retained. Suggestions from teachers and students encouraged me to add the following features in this expanded six-level series:

- **New songs**, including pop favorites from the 1960s, 1970s, 1980s and 1990s

- **International flavor** and **multi-cultural focus**, including songs and artists from around the world

- **Extensive Learning Ideas** and **Exercises** for each song

- **Photos and bios of composers and artists**, from Gloria Estefan and Billie Holiday to Michael Jackson and John Lennon

- **Newly-recorded cassettes**, especially arranged and performed by the SING IT! musicians, for classroom and home use. Cassettes contain full music, lyrics, and spoken introductions for each song.

Out of many possible songs, eighty specific ones were selected for the following reasons:

- **Enjoyment.** The melodies are often familiar and can be sung easily by individuals or groups. The accompanying cassettes provide a professional back-up that invites people to sing along easily. The music is up-beat and fun to follow.

- **Clarity.** The words of the songs introduce and reinforce vocabulary and grammatical patterns in a meaningful and easy-to-remember context. The lyrics appear both in the Text/Workbook and on the cassettes. Words on the cassettes are crisp and clear, yet follow natural pronunciation.

- **Learning value.** The songs have been carefully chosen to illustrate particular verb tenses, grammatical structures and vocabulary. Each song has a listing of the Key Structures and Communicative Objectives as well as Teaching and Learning Ideas and exercises.

The eighty songs are sequenced according to grammar and vocabulary, progressing from elementary to more advanced English. Each level, consisting of a Text/Workbook and Cassette, contains songs focusing on specific verb tenses and grammatical usages:

- **Level One:** Present Tense (verb to be + others), Imperative, Future with "going to"

- **Level Two:** Present Continuous, Future with "'ll," "will" and "shall"

- **Level Three:** Simple Past; Comparisons ("like," "as," comparative and superlative adjectives)

- **Level Four:** Other Past Tenses (Past Continuous, Present Perfect, Past Perfect)

- **Level Five:** Conditionals, If, Modals, Wish

- **Level Six:** Grand review of all verb tenses; Clauses, Non-standard English, Complete Index.

See the **Special Notes** sections which follow for more specific information on using SING IT! LEARN ENGLISH THROUGH SONG as a student or teacher. Have fun, whether you are in class or learning English on your own!

SING IT! LEARN ENGLISH THROUGH SONG is for you:

- to enjoy

- to improve your listening skills

- to increase your vocabulary

- to sharpen your pronunciation

- to improve your speaking ability

- to enliven your knowledge and use of grammatical structures

- to heighten your memory

- to make you more comfortable with use of expressions, phrases and slang

- to challenge your creativity

Twenty-five years ago I discovered that songs helped me learn a new language. Now scientists say that what I found out by personal experience is true. They say that songs enter our brains in a different way than spoken or printed things, that they go to a different part of the brain, and that they often sink in there deeply. That is why you may suddenly remember a phrase from a song that you haven't heard since you were much younger. Furthermore, scientific tests reveal that when both hemispheres of the brain are working at the same time, as they are when you participate in learning a song, the learning is more complete and longer-lasting.

In SING IT! LEARN ENGLISH THROUGH SONG, I invite you to learn English more easily and more enjoyably in a manner that will stay with you for years. I hope you have fun as you learn!

You can use SING IT! LEARN ENGLISH THROUGH SONG in many ways:

- to begin, extend or end a class

- to illustrate a particular structure you are introducing

- to reinforce and review material that you have already taught

- as a take-off point for class discussion or for oral presentations by individual students or groups of students. For example: "What song in your country does this remind you of?" "Can you tell me more about a particular song you like?", etc.

- as a lead-in for compositions, essay questions or creative writing.

You can use the cassettes to introduce and to practice the songs in the classroom. In **Special Notes for Students** and **Special Notes for Students without Teachers** which follow this section, ideas on how to use the cassettes for active listening are given.

You can also encourage students to listen to the spoken **Introductions** and songs on their own, and then practice by repeating the Introductions and singing the songs along with the cassette. Students may practice with each other or alone, in class and at home.

A complete listing of the **Key Structures** used in each song is included so that you may select a song according to what you wish to teach on a particular day. In Key Structures we include verb usages, other grammar, expressions and sometimes also key vocabulary. Look for Key Structures as they appear in song lyrics; they are highlighted in color. Verb usages are always listed first in Key Structures sections. Other grammatical structures appear in alphabetical order after verb usages. You may want to teach the structure before the class hears the song, or after. Either way works.

The listing of **Communicative Objectives** tells you, at a glance, topics and structures that you can develop and practice in conversation and in writing.

The **Learning Ideas** provide an opportunity for you to help expand students' vocabulary, to test their understanding of the content of the song and to learn new grammatical structures.

Beginning with Level Three, we add reading comprehension and focused listening exercises to invite students to stretch their skills. In the listening exercises, it is very important that the students really listen to the songs rather than find answers by looking at the printed text. The exercises and activities in Level Three are, in general, more challenging. As in the previous levels, some of the exercises invite students to work on their own; others promote class interaction. We suggest that students use their dictionaries to a greater extent, and that they keep a personal notebook with sections for new words, irregular and phrasal verbs. Level Three includes an Appendix which lists irregular verbs used in this level.

You do not need to assign all of the exercises in the Learning Ideas sections; feel free to adapt them or invent your own. Invite students to make up their own questions and answers. If you wish, you may use the Learning Ideas as homework assignments, or for a group of students to complete as you are working with another part of the class. Note that the Extra Learning sections may be too difficult for some students. We include them as an extra challenge for eager members of your class.

An **Answer Key** is available as a supplement to this book.

Footnotes help explain certain difficult words or structures. For example, the word *gonna* is numbered (1) and explained with a footnote as the reduction of *going to*. Also, when a more difficult verb tense appears in a simpler song, it is briefly explained in a footnote.

Obviously, songs are written by poets and are not designed to teach English—but learning English through song adds variety and challenge for teacher and student. Even though a song appears in Level One, it may contain a few words or structures that are more difficult. Likewise, a song in Level Six may contain some simpler tenses and vocabulary. This need not be a problem! When exposed to difficult structures and vocabulary, students often have fun trying to infer meaning from the context. Likewise, more advanced students enjoy recognizing basic structures embedded in more challenging ones.

The four **Indexes** are designed to help you and your students. Use them yourself to find songs to illustrate particular points of grammar or to choose a theme for class discussion. Show your students how to use the Indexes (fuller suggestions are given in the **Special Notes for Students** section). Have them practice looking up an artist or song. This provides good experience in alphabetizing, using telephone books, and doing research.

If you have a mixed-level class, or decide to bring several classes together for an occasion, songs are a good way to involve students of various levels at the same time. The elementary students can listen, sing along and pick up new knowledge. The more advanced students have the chance to "teach" and demonstrate their understanding to the rest of the class.

You may choose a song from any section simply because it appeals to you or your class, or because you are practicing a particular structure. Feel free to move around between the levels and use songs as you wish.

SPECIAL NOTES FOR STUDENTS

When I was trying to learn a new language—Spanish—I had a very difficult time. I paid attention in class and did my homework, but I still had a hard time pronouncing words correctly and remembering verb structures and grammar. To relax and give my brain a break, I began listening to songs from Spanish-speaking countries on the radio and on cassettes. Before I knew it, I was beginning to understand certain phrases and was able to sing along with little portions of the songs.

I decided to ask my teacher to help me out. I said to her, "If I record some songs in Spanish, will you help me figure out the parts that I don't understand?" She agreed to the idea. So, day after day, I listened to my favorite songs, and, day after day, I began learning more Spanish.

At first, I chose easier songs because I couldn't understand songs with too many words or verbs that were very difficult. Gradually my Spanish grew. Then one week in class we were trying to learn the subjunctive and I just couldn't get it. That night I happened to listen to the song "Bésame Mucho" and I heard the words ". . .como si fuera. . ." and I realized, "Ah, so that's the subjunctive!" I have never forgotten it.

So that is why, when I began teaching English, I decided to use songs as part of my teaching. My students came from many different countries: Brazil, Czechoslovakia, China, Colombia, France, Greece, Italy, Israel, Japan, Kenya, Mexico, Panama, Peru, Poland, Portugal, Puerto Rico, Russia, Spain, Surinam, Turkey, Venezuela, and even more countries. I was surprised that my students from Korea knew "Oh, Susanna!" and that a dentist from Czechoslovakia loved "Clementine." Spanish and Japanese students wanted to sing songs by The Beatles and by Simon and Garfunkel. Songs proved to be a common medium for language-learning among us.

Today, my students from Brazil and China know "From a Distance" and "We Are the World." Students from Spanish-speaking countries know and love songs by Gloria Estefan and the Miami Sound Machine. All my students learn more English as they sing songs together.

For SING IT! LEARN ENGLISH THROUGH SONG, I picked songs that I like and that students from many different countries asked me to include. I know that these particular songs are good for teaching English.

So, how should you use these songs to learn English? First of all, let's look at the various parts of the SING IT! program, and I will tell you about each part.

Contents of each level:

Level One focuses on the Present Tense (verb **to be** + others), Imperative, Future with "going to," and also includes adjectives and adverbs, definite and indefinite articles, colors and numbers, parts of the body, prepositions, and related grammar and vocabulary.

Level Two highlights Present Continuous, Future Tenses with "'ll," "shall," and "will," related grammar and vocabulary, plus a review of the Present Tenses.

Level Three features the Simple Past Tense and Comparisons ("like," "as," comparative and superlative adjectives), related grammar and vocabulary, as well as a review of the Present and Future Tenses.

Level Four focuses on other Past Tenses (Past Continuous, Present Perfect, Present Perfect Continuous, Past Perfect), and related grammar and vocabulary.

Level Five highlights Conditionals, If, Modals, Wish and more difficult grammar and vocabulary.

Level Six features a grand review of all Verb Tenses, Clauses, Non-standard English, and a Complete Index of the usages in all six levels.

As you can see, the levels progress from elementary to more difficult learning. The various parts of each level, such as the Introductions and Learning Ideas, also progress from easier to more difficult.

Remember, however, that songwriters like to have fun with words, so they do not usually limit themselves to one tense or one particular grammatical point! Because of this, you may find a few difficult parts in the early songs, and some easy parts in the more advanced sections.

Songs

Each song contains many features which are useful for learning: an Introduction, listing of Key Structures and Communicative Objectives, the Music and Song Lyrics, and Learning Ideas to enhance and challenge your comprehension of the language and words of the song.

- The **Introduction** tells you something about the song, the composers, the artists who originally performed it, and, often, some related cultural or historical background. The Introduction is repeated on the cassette, so you can listen to spoken English to improve your listening skills, and then say it back to see how your speaking compares with the person on the cassette.

- **Key Structures** tell you which structures and usages are important in the song. For each Key Structure, you will see one or more examples as they appear in the song and in the Song Lyrics themselves. By paying attention to this material, you can learn something new or sharpen your knowledge of already-learned structures.

- **Communicative Objectives** let you know different topics that you can practice talking and writing about, and what you can expect to know how to do when you complete your study of each song.

- The **Music** and complete **Song Lyrics** invite you to listen actively, look and sing along with the artists. For those of you who read music, we include the first verse and chorus with the written music. Then for your ease in studying, we include the first verse of the songs with the music, followed by the complete lyrics under the written music. If you play guitar or piano, you can follow the notes and chords to accompany the songs.

- **Learning Ideas** are designed especially to add to your fun as you move through each level. These sections have four specific parts:

  - **Vocabulary** so that you can pick out new words and use them.

  - **Questions about the Song** so that you can test your understanding of the song and the lyrics.

  - **Questions for You** to invite you to think of your own ideas and write them down.

  - **Extra Learning** to expand your knowledge and to challenge you to learn even more. Some of these questions may be too difficult for you. If they are, come back to them later when your English is more advanced.

Some songs also have **Footnotes** which explain difficult material.

Indexes

At the end of the book are four sections which make it easier for you to find things: indexes of songs by Artist, by Genre/Theme, by Grammatical Usage, and by Song Title.

- **Artist Index:** You may want to find a song that John Lennon composed, or that Stevie Wonder sang. You can look in the Artist Index for the last name of the artist to see what songs are included. For example, under John Lennon, you will see "Imagine," and find that it is on page 1.

- **Genre/Theme Index:** Suppose you want to hear a folk song, or maybe you want your class to talk about holidays. You can look in the Genre/Theme Index to see which songs focus on these themes. If you look under Holidays, you will find two songs, the names of the songs, and what pages they are on.

- **Grammatical Index:** Maybe you want to practice the Past Tense with the modal "can." Look this up in the Grammatical Index. You will find "No one could save her" from the song "Cockles and Mussels," page 40, and also "I could say" from the song "Frenesí," page 77.

- **Song Index:** This is the index you will probably use most often, so we put it at the end of the book where you can refer to it easily. Are you looking for the song "Georgia on My Mind"? Look under "G" and you will see the song listed, located on page 14.

The Text/Workbook for Level Six has a complete index of all six levels.

Answer Key

Your Text/Workbook contains an Answer Key if you are using SING IT! LEARN ENGLISH THROUGH SONG without a teacher. It provides answers to the specific questions in Learning Ideas.

A final note: you may use SING IT! LEARN ENGLISH THROUGH SONG for simple enjoyment and for learning, inside or outside the classroom.

SPECIAL NOTES FOR STUDENTS WITHOUT TEACHERS

If you are not taking English classes now, or do not have your own teacher, you may want to follow these suggestions:

1. Select a specific song.
    The **Table of Contents** and **Indexes** will help you choose a song according to your interest or according to the area of usage you want to practice.

2. On your cassette recorder, play the spoken introduction to the song. Listen without looking at the words. Listen, in a relaxed way, but with curiosity to see how much you can understand. This active listening sharpens your discriminatory skills and stretches your learning capacities. Repeat this several times.

3. Now open your Text/Workbook and look at the **Introduction**
    How many words did you hear correctly? Write them down. Which words surprise you? Write them down.

4. Play the Introduction again and silently read along with it.
    Now try saying the words along with the person on the tape. Do this as many times as you wish. Each time you do this, you can gain confidence and skill. Listen to the rhythm of the words and try to match it.

5. Look at the **Key Structures** in the Text/Workbook to give yourself a preview of the song.

6. Now close your book and play the song.
    Follow the suggestions for listening that are noted above in 2.

7. Ask yourself:
    What is this song about? What do I understand? Which words or parts don't I understand? Can I understand the unfamiliar words better if I think about the words that come before and after them?

8. Write down words and phrases that you understand.

9. Replay the entire song.
    Ask yourself: Do I understand more of the song now?

10. Play the first phrase.
    Listen to it and repeat it. Do as often as necessary.

11. Continue in the same way with the other phrases.
    Let yourself breathe and relax as you listen. You may even want to lie on the floor and stretch out, or dance and move as you hear the song.

12. Now open your Text/Workbook again and look at the words as you listen to the complete song.
    How many of them did you guess right? Which ones surprise you?

13. Look at the **Communicative Objectives.**
    If you are studying with someone, look for ways that you can practice each objective, both in conversation and in writing. If you are studying by yourself, create your own ways of practicing and developing each objective. Use your previous notes, your dictionary and your own good instincts to help you.

14. Do the **Vocabulary** exercises in your Text/Workbook.
    Be sure to write down carefully the new words you are learning.

15. Sing the entire song along with the cassette.
    Do this as many times as you wish. You can proceed one verse at a time, or, if you are in the mood, sing the whole song.

16. Write the answers to the **Questions about the song.**
    If you are not sure of an answer, go back to the song to look for ideas.

17. Write in the answers to the **Questions for you.** Use your creativity and imagination as you fill in these answers.

18. Study the **Extra Learning** sections and fill in the answers to the exercises. You do not need to do all of these exercises at one sitting. Sometimes it helps your learning to take a relaxation break. Walk around and stretch, look out a window, and then simply play the song again for enjoyment. Now go back to finish another part of the Extra Learning sections.

19. Verify your answers to the specific questions by checking with the **Answer Key**. Before looking at the answers, be sure you write down your own responses in your Text/Workbook. Then check them by looking at the **Answer Key.**

Have fun being your own teacher. See how much you can learn on your own. Give yourself a good grade when you do a particularly successful lesson.

You may enjoy listening to the songs as you take the bus or drive to work or school, as you do things around your home or at the beach, or before you go to bed. The songs slip into your brain unconsciously. Before you know it, you will be humming along, then singing along in English.

ACKNOWLEDGMENTS AND THANKS

I want to thank:

Eric A. Anderson and Bob Briar at Cutler's Records in New Haven, Connecticut; the Bales-Gitlin crew, Roni Bruskin, Gordon Emerson, Molly Fleming, John Forster, Jeff Fuller, Cliff Furnald, Les Julian, Sal Libro, Jon Russell and Pete Seeger for their musical input and enthusiasm.

Alexis Johnson, Caroline Gear, Tim Rees, and all the instructors and students at the International Language Institute of Massachusetts, Inc.; Jan Hortas and instructors and students at Yale English Language Institute; Marian Knight and all at ELS Language Center at Albertus Magnus College in New Haven, Connecticut; Karen Serret of the Bilingual Program in Waterbury, Connecticut; Bob Nelson of City College of San Francisco; Lyn Jacob and Jane Larson of the Instituto de Estudios Norteamericanos in Barcelona and all past students and teachers there, especially ex-director Bob Ramsey—for helping shape the contents and direction of SING IT! LEARN ENGLISH THROUGH SONG.

Jane Baron Rechtman, Lee Bergman, Bruce P. Blair, my Bloom family—Paul, Noah, Josh, Miriam and Martha—Jason Bohannon, Larry Cerri, Eric Chen, Maureen E. Daly, Kathy Davis, Joe FitzGerald, Jacqueline Flamm, Ethel Granick, John Holland, Jean Kerr, Lynn Johnson-Martin, Zarah Johnson-Morris, Michael Lerner, Sheila Lirio, Linda McGuire, Marga Mueller, George W. Nowacki, Randi Parker, Ilana Rubenfeld and my Rubenfeld Synergy friends, Liz Sader, Mitsue Sakamoto, Wendy Samberg, Angelyn Singer, Paul Spector, Jesse Sugarmann, Cheryl R. Wiener, Jianxin Yang, Hongbo Zang—for their ongoing consultation and support.

My editor Louise Jennewine for her thorough dedication and good humor, Janet Gomolson for her unstinting enthusiasm, Fred Perkins for believing in SING IT! way back then and now, and Lowell Britson for stepping in to help us out.

Special thanks to my own Kentucky family and to all the people around the world who have taught me songs and learned songs from me.

Millie Grenough

ACKNOWLEDGMENTS FOR SONGS

We have made every effort to determine the copyright status of the songs included in this book. We wish to thank the publishers of the following songs for permission to reprint their copyrighted material.

"Anything You Can Do" by Irving Berlin. Copyright © 1946 Irving Berlin. Copyright renewed. International copyright secured. Used by permission. All rights reserved.

"Frenesí" by Alberto Domínguez. English words by Ray Charles & S. K. Russell. Copyright © 1939 & 1941 by Peer International Corporation. Copyrights renewed. International copyright secured. All rights reserved. Used by permission.

"Georgia on My Mind" by Hoagy Carmichael and Stuart Gorrell. Copyright © 1930 by Peer International Corporation. Copyright renewed 1957 by Peer International Corporation. Copyright 1980 by Peer International Corporation. Controlled in Australia and New Zealand by Allan & Co., Ltd., Melbourne. International copyright secured. Made in USA. All rights reserved.

"I Just Called to Say I Love You" by Stevie Wonder. Copyright © 1984 Jobete Music Co., Inc. and Black Bull Music, Inc. International copyright secured. Made in USA. All rights reserved.

"Imagine" by John Lennon. Copyright © 1971 Lenono Music. All rights administered by Sony Music Publishing, 8 Music Square West, Nashville, Tennessee 37203. Used by permission.

"Lemon Tree" Words and Music by Will Holt. © 1960 Lemon Tree Music, Inc. (ASCAP). Copyright renewed 1988. All rights reserved. Used by permission.

"Oh, What a Beautiful Mornin'" (from "Oklahoma!"). Lyrics by Oscar Hammerstein II. Music by Richard Rodgers. Copyright © 1943 by WILLIAMSON MUSIC CO. Copyright renewed. WILLIAMSON MUSIC owner of publication and allied rights throughout the world. International copyright secured. All rights reserved.

"What a Wonderful World" by George David Weiss, Bob Thiele. © 1967 Range Road Music Inc. and Quartet Music Inc. Used by permission. All rights reserved.

Our appreciation to the staff of the Archive of Folk Songs of the Library of Congress in Washington, D.C., and the staff of the New Haven Public Library for their assistance. The following songs were adapted from field recordings in the Archive of American Folk Songs in Washington, D.C., and from other public domain material: "Clementine," "Cockles and Mussels," "Oh, Susanna!" (words and music by Stephen Foster), "On Top of Old Smoky," "The Twelve Days of Christmas," "When I First Came to this Land" (traditional; lyrics translated by Oscar Brand; from Singing Holidays by Oscar Brand, 1957; used courtesy of Alfred A. Knopf).

John Lennon, the composer of "Imagine."   *UPI/Bettmann*

"Y ou may say I'm a dreamer, but I'm not the only one..." The lyrics of this song paint a world where people live together in harmony, where there are no enemies, where people share the riches they have with each other.

John Lennon, the composer of "Imagine," was[1] one of the key members of the English group The Beatles. He helped[1] open new horizons in popular music. This is one of the best-known[2] and most-loved[2] songs for peace in the English-speaking[2] world. Yoko Ono, the widow of John Lennon, graciously gives us permission to use the song in this book.

[1] **was, helped:** past tense of **is, help**
[2] **best-known, most-loved, English-speaking:** hyphenated adjectives

KEY STRUCTURES

- **Review of Present and Future Tenses, Imperative, Contractions, Prepositions, "There"**

- **Verb + "er" = Noun**   I'm a **dreamer**

COMMUNICATIVE OBJECTIVES

- to talk about imagination

- to plan your own dreams for the world and discuss them

Imagine

Words and music by JOHN LENNON

1. Im-ag-ine there's no heav-en,_____ it's eas-y if you_____ try,_____

— No hell_ be-low us,_____ a-bove us on-ly sky.

— Im-ag-ine all_ the peo - ple_____

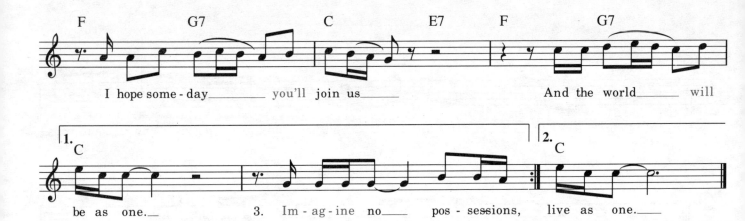

I hope some-day_____ you'll join us_____ And the world_____ will

1. C be as one.__ **3.** Im-ag-ine no__ pos-sessions, **2.** C live as one.__

 SONG LYRICS

1. **Imagine there's**[3] no heaven—**it's**[3] easy if you try,—
   No hell **below** us, **above** us only sky.
   Imagine all the people livin'[4] for today, I-hi[5].

2. **Imagine there's** no countries[6], it **isn't**[3] hard to do,
   Nothing to kill or die for, and no religion too[6].
   Imagine all the people living life in peace, yoo hoo[5].

   CHORUS: You may say[7] **I'm**[3] a **dreamer**, but **I'm** not the only one.
              I hope some day **you'll**[3] join us and the world **will be** as one.

3. **Imagine** no possessions, I wonder if you can,
   No need for greed or hunger, a brotherhood of man. Oh,
   Imagine all the people sharing all the world, yoo hoo.

   CHORUS: You may say[7] **I'm**[3] a **dreamer**, Oh-ho but **I'm** not the only one.
              I hope some day **you'll**[3] join us and the world **will live** as one.

[3]**there's, it's, isn't, I'm, you'll:** contractions of **there is, it is, is not, I am, you will**
[4]**livin':** reduction of **living**
[5]**I-hi, yoo hoo:** vocal sounds
[6]**there's no countries, no religion too:** poetic license used for rhythm and rhyme. In correct English, **there are no countries, no religion either**
[7]**may:** modal. **You may say:** It is possible to say. See Level Five for more examples.

4

- *Vocabulary*

  1. In this song, which words are new for you? Write them down. Can you use them in sentences?
  2. Crossword Puzzle. All of the words are from the song.

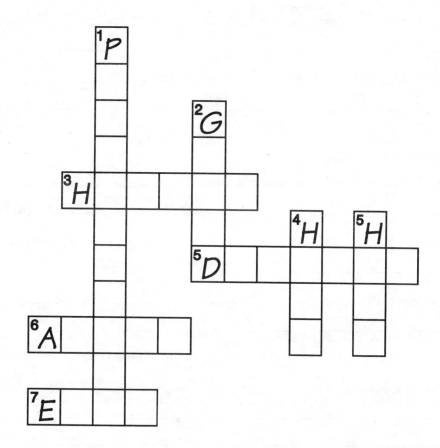

Across

3. place of perfect happiness in the afterlife
5. one who imagines wonderful things
6. opposite of below
7. opposite of hard

Down

1. things that someone owns
2. excessive possessiveness
4. It isn't _____ to do.
5. place of misery in the afterlife

- *Questions about the song*

Listen to the song and put these words in the correct order. Use correct punctuation and capitalization.

1. a   dreamer   say   may   I'm   you   _You may say I'm a dreamer._

   _____

2. us   day   some   you'll   hope   I   join   _____

   _____

3. you   I   can   if   wonder   _____

   _____

4. world   the   sharing   people   all   the   Imagine   all   _____

   _____

- *Questions for you*

   1. Write down two things you imagine for yourself: _____

      _____

   2. For your family: _____

      _____

   3. For your city: _____

      _____

      _____

   4. For the world: _____

      _____

      _____

Discuss and compare your answers with a partner.

- *Extra Learning*

   Verb + "er" = Noun

   Write sentences using words that end in -er. Follow the example.

   1. Ken thinks about philosophical problems. _He's a thinker._

      _____

2. Manuel always dreams about beautiful places and wonderful people. _____

    _____

3. Louise swims four miles a day five days a week. _____

    _____

4. Suzie sings her scales every day. _____

    _____

5. Carmen hikes in the woods and on mountain trails. _____

    _____

Laurey (Shirley Jones) and Curly (Gordon MacRae) enjoy the fresh air in "Oklahoma!".

Springer/Bettmann Film Archive

This song is from the musical "Oklahoma!" by Richard Rodgers and Oscar Hammerstein II. The lyrics have many reductions (shortened forms of words) to give the song a relaxed, easy feeling. The composers also let the singers sing in non-standard English to show that they are ordinary ("down-home") people.

As you sing, imagine spacious farmland, clear blue skies, and crisp clean air.

KEY STRUCTURES

- **Comparisons**

    "as" + Adjective + "as"   The corn is **as high as** an elephant's eye

    "like" + Noun   cattle are standin' **like statues**

- **Non-standard English**

    it **looks like** it's climbin'   it **looks as if** it's climbin'

    it **don't** miss a tree   it **doesn't** miss a tree

    I got a beautiful feeling   **I've got...** or **I have**

    ol' weepin' willer   **old weeping willow** (tree)

- **Review of Present and Present Continuous Tenses, Reductions**

COMMUNICATIVE OBJECTIVES

- to express comparisons

- to discuss city and country living

- to give reasons for your preferences

Oh, What a Beautiful Mornin'

Words by OSCAR HAMMERSTEIN II
Music by RICHARD RODGERS

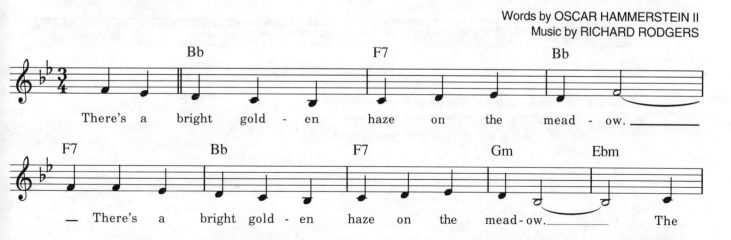

There's a bright gold - en haze on the mead - ow. _____

— There's a bright gold - en haze on the mead - ow. _____ The

corn is as high as an el - e - phant's eye, An' it
looks like it's climb - in' clear up to the sky.

CHORUS:

Oh, what a beau - ti - ful morn - in';

Oh, what a beau - ti - ful day.

I got a beau - ti - ful feel - in'

Ev - 'ry - thing's go - in' my way.

🎼 **SONG LYRICS**

1. There's a bright golden haze on the meadow.   REPEAT
   The corn is **as high as** an elephant's eye,
   An'[1] it **looks like** it's[2] climbin'[1] clear up to the sky.

[1]**An', climbin'**: reductions of **and, climbing**
[2]**it's**: contraction of **it is**

CHORUS: Oh, what a beautiful mornin'[3];
                Oh, what a beautiful day.
                I got[5] a beautiful feelin'[3]
                Ev'rything's[4] goin'[3] my way.

2. All the cattle **are standin'**[3] **like statues**.   **REPEAT**
   They **don't**[4] **turn** their heads as they see me ride by.
   But a little brown mav'rick[6] **is winkin'**[3] her eye.   **CHORUS**

3. All the sounds of the earth are like music.   **REPEAT**
   The breeze is so busy **it don't miss** a tree,
   And an **ol'**[3] **weepin'**[3] **willer is laughin'**[3] at me.

           CHORUS +   Oh, what a beautiful day.

LEARNING IDEAS

- *Vocabulary*

   1. In this song, which words are new for you? Write them down. Can you use them in sentences?
   2. Unscramble these words from the song. The first letter of each word is provided in the center column. Then match them with their meanings on the right.

   _E_   1. doweam   m _eadow_____   A. pleasing to look at

   ____   2. zeah   h _____   B. four-legged farm animals

   ____   3. ttalce   c _____   C. light vapor or smoke in the atmosphere

   ____   4. luuifbaet b _____   D. cryin'

   ____   5. zeeerb   b _____   E. level grassland

   ____   6. n'peewi w _____   F. a light, gentle wind

[3]**Mornin', feelin', goin', standin', winkin', ol', weepin', ɩaughin'**: reductions of **morning, feeling, going, standing, winking, old, weeping, laughing**
[4]**Ev'rything's, don't**: contractions of **Everything is, do not**
[5]**I got: I've got = I have**. See "He's Got The Whole World" in Level One and "I Want to Hold Your Hand" in Level Two for other examples.
[6]**mav'rick**: an unbranded animal on the range (from Samuel Maverick, a U.S. pioneer who did not brand his calves); can also mean a person who does not conform to the usual rules.

- *Questions about the song*

   Listen to the song. Find the ten errors in the sentences below. Circle them and then write in the correct word above your circles. Listen to the song again and re-write each line correctly.

   1. There's a (dark) golden (cloud) on the (river.)

      There's a bright golden haze on the meadow.

   2. All the horses are eatin' like pigs.

      _____

   3. They don't shake their tails as they hear us walk by.

      _____

- *Questions for you*

   1. Describe the place where you live. Tell what life is like there. _____

      _____

      _____

      _____

      _____

   2. Do you prefer living in the city or living in the country? _____

      _____

      Give two reasons for your preference. _____

      _____

      _____

      _____

- *Extra Learning*

   Comparisons: "as" + Adjective + "as"

   1. What is as high as an elephant's eye? _____ .
   2. Make up your own sentences.

      _____ is as sweet as _____ .

      _____ is as difficult as _____ .

      _____ is as _____ as _____ .

Comparisons: "like" + Noun

1. How are the cattle standing? _____ .

2. Make up your own sentences:
    The Amazon River is like _____ .

    New York City is like _____ .

    Mount Fuji is like _____ .

    _____ is like _____ .

"There" as Subject

Can you describe your classroom in three sentences? Begin each sentence with "There...

1. _____ .

2. _____ .

3. _____ .

Michael Bolton with
his Grammy Award.

Reuters/Bettmann

Ray Charles at the piano.

UPI/Bettmann

This song is from the 1930s, but it was[1] in 1960 that the blind singer and piano player Ray Charles made[2] it famous. Thirty-one years later, in 1991, a singer named Michael Bolton made a new recording of "Georgia on My Mind" and won[3] an award for his record.

Is Georgia a person? Or is Georgia a state in the southern part of the United States? Whichever it is, the person singing this song is homesick for Georgia and wants to be with her or wants to be there.

See "Deep in the Heart of Texas" in Level One for another "homesick" song.

[1] **was:** past tense of **is**
[2] **made:** past of **make**
[3] **won:** past of **win**

KEY STRUCTURES

- **Phrasal Verbs**   arms **reach out**, road **leads back**

- **Noun + "ful" = Adjective**   in **peaceful** dreams I see

- **Review of Present Tense, "As" + Adjective + "As"**

COMMUNICATIVE OBJECTIVES

- to talk about home and about being "homesick"

- to describe various people and places in detail

Georgia On My Mind

Words by STUART GORRELL
Music by HOAGY CARMICHAEL

sweet and clear as moon-light through the pines.___

BRIDGE:

Oth-er arms reach out to me; Oth-er eyes smile ten-der-ly;___

Still in peace---ful dreams I see___ the road leads back to you.

3. Geor-gia,___ Geor-gia,___ no peace I find. Just an

old sweet song keeps Geor-gia on my mind.___

SONG LYRICS

1. Georgia, Georgia, the whole day through,
   Just an old sweet song **keeps** Georgia on my mind, Georgia on my mind.

2. Georgia, Georgia, a song of you
   Comes as sweet and clear as moonlight through the pines.

   BRIDGE: Other arms **reach out** to me; other eyes **smile** tenderly;
   Still in **peaceful** dreams I **see** the road **leads back** to you.

3. Georgia, Georgia, no peace I **find**.
   Just an old sweet song **keeps** Georgia on my mind.

LEARNING IDEAS

- *Vocabulary*

  1. In this song, which words are new for you? Write them down. Can you use them in sentences?

  2. Crossword Puzzle. All of the words are from the song.

Across

3. maintains
5. opposite of sunlight
6. calm, quiet
7. opposite of new

Down

1. how sugar tastes
2. in a soft, caring way
4. music with words
6. evergreen trees

- *Questions about the song*

  1. What keeps Georgia on the singer's mind? _____

  _____

  2. Do you think this song is about a woman named Georgia or the state of Georgia?

  _____

  Give two reasons for your answer. _____

  _____

  _____

- *Questions for you*

  1. Describe a place where there are pine trees. _____

     _____

  2. From your home, what can you see in the moonlight? _____

     _____

  3. Write down two "sweet and clear" memories of your birthplace. _____

     _____

     _____

  4. Do you have any clear memories of someone you love who is far away?

     Write down the person's name and two memories. _____

     _____

     _____

     _____

- *Extra Learning*

  Noun + "ful" = Adjective

  Work with a partner to ask and answer the following questions with complete sentences.
  The first time around, you ask the questions and your partner responds. The second time,
  your partner asks and you respond. To answer, use the words in the box, or add your own.
  There is no "correct" answer; your answer depends on your own experience.

awful	beautiful	peaceful	wonderful

  1. Q. When you hear your favorite song, how do you feel?

     A. _____

     Q. Why do you feel that way?

     A. _____

2. Q. When you see a beautiful sunrise, how do you feel?

   A. _____

   Q. Why?

   A. _____

3. Q. When you say good-bye to your best friend, how do you feel?

   A. _____

   Q. Why?

   A. _____

Phrasal (two-word) verbs

Choose a two-word verb from the box to complete each sentence. Be sure to use the correct form of the verb.

go through	grow up	lead back	let in	reach out

1. When my dad _____ his arms, my baby brother always runs towards him.

2. This road seems to be going in a circle. I think it _____ to New York.

3. I want my children to _____ in a beautiful place.

4. Do you have to _____ Chicago to get to San Francisco from Detroit?

5. Will you ask Alan to _____ the dog, please?

Louis ("Satchmo") Armstrong at a live performance.   *Springer/Bettmann Film Archive*

Louis Armstrong sings this song in the background of the movie "Good Morning, Vietnam." He invites us all to make this world a place where it is safe for people to walk down the street, shake hands and say, "How do you do!"

Louis Armstrong was born in 1900 in New Orleans, Louisiana. He was sent[1] to a home for boys when he was 13, and it was there that he learned to play the horn. The other boys began calling him "Satchel[2]-mouth" because of his big mouth. Later this name was shortened[1] to the nickname[2] "Satchmo."

Louis was one of the greatest influences on the development of jazz music. When he died at the age of 71, many people throughout the world mourned the passing of this great man with his unique voice and talent.

---

[1]**was sent, was shortened**: past tense, passive voice of **send** and **shorten**. See Level Four for more examples.
[2]**satchel**: a traveling or school book bag; **nickname**: a familiar or affectionate name for someone or something

KEY STRUCTURES

- **Comparative with "more than"**   They'll learn much **more than** I'll ever know

- **Emphasis words**   **also, ever, much, really, so, too, yes**

- **Reflexive Pronoun**   I think to **myself**

- **Verb + Object + Verb**   **I see them bloom, watch them grow**

- **Review of Present, Present Continuous and Future Tenses, Adjectives, Colors, Gerunds, Reductions**

COMMUNICATIVE OBJECTIVES

- to greet people in various ways

- to discuss what you see and what you think

What a Wonderful World

Words and music by GEORGE DAVID WEISS and BOB THIELE

1. I see trees of green, red ros - es too. I see them bloom

for me and you,____ and I think____ to my - self,

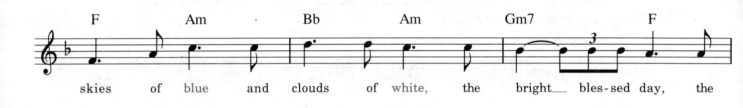

BRIDGE:

C7   F

al - so   on   the   fac - es   of   peo - ple pass - in' by.   I   see

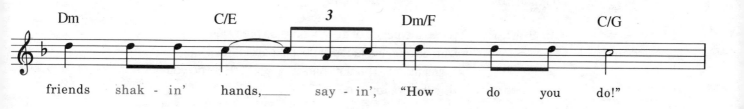

Dm   C/E   *3*   Dm/F   C/G

friends shak - in'   hands,___ say - in', "How   do   you   do!"

Dm/F   *3*   F#dim   Gm7   F#dim   C7   *D.S. al fine*

But they're real - ly say - in',   "I   love   you." 3. I   hear

♪ SONG LYRICS

1. I **see** trees of **green**, **red** roses too.
   I **see them bloom** for me and you,
   And I **think to myself**, "What a wonderful world."

2. I **see** skies of **blue** and clouds of **white**,
   The bright blessed day, the dark sacred night,
   And I **think to myself**, "What a wonderful world."

   BRIDGE: I **see** the colors of the rainbow, so pretty in the sky,
   Are also on the faces of people passin'[3] by.
   I **see** friends **shakin'**[3] hands, **sayin'**[3], "How do you do!"
   But they**'re** really **sayin'**[3], "I love you."

3. I **hear babies cry**, I **watch them grow.**
   They**'ll**[4] **learn much more than** I**'ll**[4] ever **know**
   And I **think to myself**, "What a wonderful world."
   Yes, I **think to myself**, "What a wonderful world."

LEARNING IDEAS

- *Vocabulary*

  1. In this song, which words are new for you? Write them down. Can you use them in sentences?

  _____

- *Questions about the song*

  1. What are three things the singer sees? _____

  _____

  _____

  2. What are two things he sees people doing? _____

  _____

  3. What does he hear them saying? _____

  _____

[3]passin', shakin', sayin': reductions of **passing, shaking, saying**
[4]They'll, I'll: contracted forms of future tense (**They will, I will**)

- *Questions for you*

  1. When you walk down the street in your neighborhood, what are two things you see? _____
  _____

  2. What do you think to yourself when you see them? _____
  _____

  3. Do people in your country shake hands or make any other physical gesture when they greet
  people? If so, what? _____
  _____

  Explain if women and men use the same greetings. _____
  _____

  Explain if children and adults use similar greetings. _____
  _____

- *Extra Learning*

  Adjectives

  What is another way to say:

  1. trees of green _____

  2. skies of blue _____

  3. clouds of white _____

  Emphasis

  The composer uses "also," "ever," "much," "really," "so," "too," and "yes" to add emphasis to his
  statements. Find these words in the song lyrics. Write your own sentences using the words below.

  1. ever _____

  2. really _____

  3. too _____

  Comparatives

  Answer the following questions with complete sentences, starting with the words "Yes" or "No."

  1. Do you know much more English now than last year? _____
  _____

  2. Does anyone in your family know more English than you? _____
  _____

3. Do you ever eat more than you need to? _____

_____

4. Do you think that Gloria Estefan will become more famous than Louis Armstrong? _____

_____

Now ask a partner these questions. Then let your partner ask you the questions, and you respond out loud. Compose three similar questions using "more than." Ask your partner to respond in writing.

1. _____

2. _____

3. _____

Greetings

Write appropriate greetings for each of the following:

1. your best friend Karl _____

2. the old lady who lives around the corner _____

3. your teacher _____

4. the president of your country _____

5. Michael Jackson _____

Now pretend that you are one of these people or a person of your choosing. Practice meeting someone; greet each other and have a conversation.

READING COMPREHENSION

TOUR FOR MUSIC-LOVERS

Rosalie and Carlos Betancourt are leaving Friday to go on a tour with a group of secondary school students. They are excited because the theme of the tour is "Modern Musicians from the British Isles." They will fly out of Caracas Friday morning, April 1, arriving in London that evening, and will leave London Sunday evening, April 10.

During their nine days, they will tour various concert places around London and pick up memorabilia[1] in Tower Records and the Virgin Megastore[1] in Piccadilly Circus. Rosalie is a John Lennon and Beatles fan. She hopes to find old photos to bring back to her friends. Carlos likes Mick Jagger and The Rolling Stones, so he will look for records that he can't find back in Caracas. Maybe they will get up to Liverpool to see where The Beatles grew up, and to Glasgow, Scotland to visit where the folksinger Donovan was born. They also want to go to Ireland to see the home cities of Enya and Bono. They hope to get tickets for shows Saturday evening in London. Carlos wants to see Madonna, even though she is not from the British Isles. Rosalie wants to see U2 and meet Bono in person. What a way to spend their last night in England! They won't get a lot of sleep that night, but they will have a lot of stories to tell their friends when they arrive the next night in Caracas.

For each statement below, circle True, False, or ? if the story doesn't say. If the statement is false, circle the errors and write in the corrections.

1. Rosalie and Carlos are traveling via Trans World Airlines.   T F ?
_____

2. They are flying with a group of university students.   T F ?
_____

3. Carlos likes The Rolling Stones.   T F ?
_____

4. Donovan was born in Liverpool, Scotland.   T F ?
_____

5. Rosalie and Carlos are twins.   T F ?
_____

6. The trip costs $1,500 per person.   T F ?
_____

7. Rosalie thinks Madonna is the world's greatest singer.   T F ?
_____

8. Rosalie and Carlos already have tickets for Saturday concerts.   T F ?
_____

[1] **memorabilia, mega- :** find these words in your dictionary and write down their meanings.

9. They will pick up memorabilia at stores in Picadilly Circus.   T F ?

_____

10. Carlos' favorite Stones' song is "As Tears Go By."   T F ?

_____

COMPARISONS

Compose questions and answers using the cue words below. Use material from the story as well as from your own imagination.

1. Group U2 / as famous as / The Rolling Stones?

   Q. _____

   A. _____

2. Madonna / sing / as _____ as / Enya?

   Q. _____

   A. _____

3. Carlos / like / Bono / as _____ as / Madonna?

   Q. _____

   A. _____

4. Rosalie / buy / as _____ records as / Carlos?

   Q. _____

   A. _____

5. Mick Jagger / look like / Madonna?

   Q. _____

   A. _____

6. you / like / _____ as much as / Michael Jackson?

   Q. _____

   A. _____

Now compose two more questions. Ask your partner to respond.

COMPOSITION

Imagine that you have your own travel agency. Design the trip of your dreams and write a brochure to advertise it. Be sure to include the price, the travel dates, means of transportation (air, train, bus, boat, and name of carrier), length of stay, who may go, what they will do, where they will stay. Make it as attractive as you can by adding photos and pictures.

A scene from the Smoky Mountains.   *The Bettmann Archive*

Old Smoky is a mountain somewhere in the state of Kentucky, but the story it tells could be from any place in the world. In this song a woman sings her sad story to warn young girls of the dangers of love. What is her message? "Don't believe everything that a man tells you!"

Boys and men may protest, "But what about women? Can we trust them any more than they can trust us?" There are many other ballads that tell that side of the story.

KEY STRUCTURES

- **Past Tense, Irregular**   **I lost**[1] my true lover

- **Comparisons**   **worse than** a thief, **more lies than** the crossties

- **Gerunds as Nouns**   **courting** is pleasure, **parting** is grief

- **Review of Present and Future Tenses, Imperative, "There"**

COMMUNICATIVE OBJECTIVES

- to talk about "true love" and "false love"

- to make normal and exaggerated comparisons

On Top of Old Smoky

Traditional mountain song

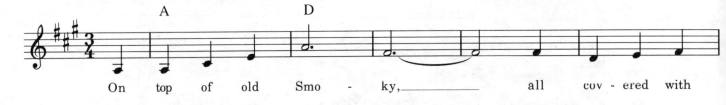

On top of old Smo - ky,_____ all cov - ered with

snow,_____ I lost my true love -

er_____ from court - ing too slow._____

[1]**lost**: past tense of **lose**

SONG LYRICS

1. On top of old Smoky, all covered with snow,
   I **lost** my true lover from **courting** too slow[2].

2. Now **courting** is pleasure and **parting** is grief,
   And a falsehearted lover is **worse than a thief**.

3. A thief **will** just **rob** you and take what you have,
   But a falsehearted lover **will lead** you to your grave.

4. Now the grave **will decay** you and turn you to dust.
   There's not one boy in a hundred that a poor girl can trust.

5. They**'ll hug** you and kiss you and tell you **more lies**
   Than the crossties[3] on a railroad or the stars in the skies.

6. So **come**, you young maidens, and **listen** to me.
   Never place your affections on a green willow tree.

7. The leaves **will wither**, the roots **will die**,
   And you**'ll all be forsaken**[4] and never know why.

LEARNING IDEAS

- *Vocabulary*

  Unscramble the words in the column on the left. Then match them with their meanings on the right.

  _E_ 1. vearg   g _rave_____   A. abandoned

  ____ 2. sssroctei c _____   B. unmarried girls or women

  ____ 3. rthewi   w _____   C. dry up

  ____ 4. naskerof   f _____   D. wooden planks on a railroad track

  ____ 5. sendaim   m _____   E. burial place, tomb

[2]**slow**: poetic license, to rhyme with snow; in correct English, adverb slowly
[3]**crossties**: the wooden planks on a railroad track
[4]**you'll all be forsaken**: future tense, passive voice

- ## *Questions about the song*

  Listen to the song. Can you put these words in order without looking at the Song Lyrics?
  Use correct punctuation.

  1. pleasure   is   grief   Now   and   parting   is   courting

  _____

  2. kiss   hug   you   They'll   you   and

  _____

  3. forsaken   why   know   all   You'll   never   be   and

  _____

  4. slow   too   courting   lost   I   lover   true   my   from

  _____

- ## *Questions for you*

  Answer in complete sentences. If possible, add details.

  1. Do you ever give advice to your friends? _____

  _____

  2. Do you ever eat ice cream for breakfast? _____

  _____

  3. When you were in elementary school, did you ever lose your schoolbooks? _____

  _____

  4. What did the person in the song lose? _____

  _____

  5. When you were a child, did you ever walk on railroad tracks? _____

  _____

  Now ask someone else these questions and see how that person's answers compare with yours.

- ## *Extra Learning*

Comparisons: Normal and Exaggerated

Comparisons can be true, or they can be exaggerated. For example, the person in this song sings, "He'll tell you more lies than stars in the skies." That's a lot of lies! Now make up your own comparisons with the following subjects. Let the first comparison be true, and the second comparison be exaggerated.

1. English exam / harder than

   True: *This English exam is harder than last year's.*

   Exaggerated: *This English exam is the hardest ever given in my country.*

2. broken leg / worse than

   True: _____

   Exaggerated: _____

3. hungry teenagers / eat more food than

   True: _____

   Exaggerated: _____

4. Michael Jackson / sings better than

   True: _____

   Exaggerated: _____

Debate

Choose two teams for a debate. One team will argue that "courting is pleasure." Another will argue that "courting is always terrible." Then debate this topic: "Love is always true" versus "Love is almost always false."

A family Christmas celebration in the 1870s.

The Bettmann Archive

In your country, do you have special days when you give gifts to other people? Some people present gifts on birthdays or saints' days. Others give and receive gifts at special seasons of the year.

Many cultures give gifts to celebrate the coming of a special God or a special person. In Christian cultures, the birth of Jesus Christ is celebrated on December 25,[1] the day called Christmas.

This song commemorates the twelve days of gift-giving between December 25 and January 6.

[1] Note that in English we say "December twenty-fifth." We write "December 25," or "25 December."

KEY STRUCTURES

- **Past Tense**   my true love **gave**[2] to me

- **Gerunds as Adjectives**   four **calling** birds, six geese **a-laying**[3] + others

- **Numbers**

  Ordinal   On the **first** day of Christmas + others

  Cardinal   **two** turtle doves + others

COMMUNICATIVE OBJECTIVES

- to talk about gift-giving and holidays

The Twelve Days of Christmas

Traditional holiday song

1. On the first day of Christ-mas, my true love gave to me a par-tridge_ in a pear

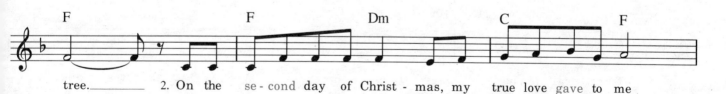

tree._____ 2. On the se-cond day of Christ-mas, my true love gave to me

(etc.)

two tur-tle doves and a par-tridge_____ in a pear tree. 3. On the

[2]**gave**: past tense of **give**
[3]**a-laying** = **laying** (extra syllable, **a-**, added to fit rhythm of music. Same for **a-swimming**, **a-milking**, etc.)

third day of Christ-mas, my true love gave to me three French hens,

two tur-tle doves, and a par-tridge in a pear tree. 4. On the

fourth day of Christ-mas, my true love gave to me four call-ing birds,
three French hens,

two tur-tle doves, and a par-tridge in a pear tree. 5. On the

F   G   C

fifth day of Christ-mas, my true love gave to me, five gold-en rings;

F   Bb   C

four call-ing birds, three French hens, two tur-tle doves, and a

F   Bb   F   C   F

par-tridge in a pear tree. 6. On the sixth day of Christ-mas, my
7. On the seventh day of Christ-mas, my

true love gave to me   six   geese   a - lay - ing, *(to 5)*   five   gold - en
true love gave to me   seven   swans   a - swim - ing, *(to 6)*

rings,   four___ call - ing birds,   three   French__ hens,

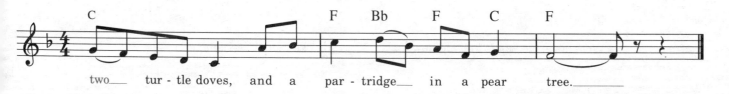

two___ tur - tle doves, and a   par - tridge__ in a pear   tree.___

SONG LYRICS

1. On the **first** day of Christmas, my true love **gave** to me
A partridge in a pear tree.

2. On the **second** day of Christmas, my true love **gave** to me
Two turtle doves and a partridge in a pear tree.

3. On the **third** day of Christmas, my true love **gave** to me
Three French hens, **two** turtle doves, and a partridge in a pear tree.

4. On the **fourth** day of Christmas, my true love **gave** to me
Four calling birds, **three** French hens, **two** turtle doves, and a partridge in a pear tree.

5. On the **fifth** day of Christmas, my true love **gave** to me

     CHORUS: **Five** golden rings, **four calling** birds, **three** French hens,
                          Two turtle doves, and a partridge in a pear tree.

6. On the **sixth** day of Christmas, my true love **gave** to me **six** geese **a-laying**,   CHORUS

7. On the **seventh** day of Christmas, my true love **gave** to me
Seven swans **a-swimming**, six geese **a-laying**,   CHORUS

8. On the **eighth** day of Christmas, my true love **gave** to me **eight** maids **a-milking**—etc[4].

9. On the **ninth** day of Christmas, my true love **gave** to me **nine** ladies **dancing**—etc.

10. On the **tenth** day of Christmas, my true love **gave** to me **ten** lords **a-leaping**—etc.

11. On the **eleventh** day of Christmas, my true love **gave** to me **eleven** pipers **piping**—etc.

12. On the **twelfth** day of Christmas, my true love **gave** to me **twelve** drummers **drumming**—etc.

LEARNING IDEAS

- *Vocabulary*

  Write down the words that are new for you. Can you use them in sentences?

- *Questions about the song*

  In this song the composer uses gerunds (verb + -**ing**) eight times to describe nouns.
  1. Can you find each of the eight gerunds and the nouns they describe?

      a-swimming swans   _____

      _____   _____

      _____   _____

      _____   _____

  2. Now reverse the order of four of them, leaving out the "**a-**" prefix.

      For example: _swans swimming_   _____

      _____   _____

  3. Now think of any four objects and choose your own gerunds to describe them.

      _____   _____

      _____   _____

- *Questions for you*

  1. What is the most festive holiday in your country? _____

      When is it? _____

[4]**etc.**: abbreviation for **et cetera** = **and so forth**

2. What do people do to celebrate it? _____

   What foods do they eat? _____

3. When is your birthday? _____

4. In your country, do people give presents to celebrate birthdays? _____

   If so, what was your favorite present and who gave it to you? _____

   _____

- ## *Extra Learning*

Calendars, Dates, Ordinal Numbers

Bring in a calendar with each month of the year. Then write in something special you intend to do in each month. Now choose three of the months and tell a friend what you plan to do in each one.

1. *February* _____ is the *second* _____ month of the year.

   On *February 14, I'll give out all my valentines.* _____

   _____

2. _____ is the _____ month of the year.

   On _____ , _____

   _____

3. _____ is the _____ month of the year.

   On _____ , _____

   _____

Now ask some friends about their calendars and dates.

Pronunciation Practice

This song is excellent for practicing many different sounds quickly. It is also a good song to stretch your memory. Listen to one line at a time, then sing it with the cassette. Do this as many times as necessary to memorize the lines.

COCKLES AND MUSSELS

A narrow street in Old Dublin.   *The Bettmann Archive*

Every country has its songs about pretty young women and the young men who fall in love with them. Sometimes they live happily ever after and sometimes the ending is not so happy. This song is an old Irish folk song, probably written[1] about 1750.

Cockles and mussels are shellfish. The pretty young woman, Molly Malone, sells these fish in the streets of Dublin, the capital city of Ireland. Listen to the song to find out what she sings as she sells her fish. You'll also discover how the story ends.

---

[1] **written**: past participle of **write**

KEY STRUCTURES

- **Past Tense**

Verb "to be"	She **was**[2] a fishmonger[3], so **were**[2] her father and mother
Regular	She **wheeled** her wheelbarrow[3] + others
Irregular	I first **set**[2] my eyes on sweet Molly Malone
Modal	No one **could**[2] **save** her

- **"As" + Clause**   **As she wheeled** her wheelbarrow

COMMUNICATIVE OBJECTIVES

- to talk about romantic stories from your country and from other countries

- to describe two or more things that happen at the same time

- to practice "tongue twisters"

Cockles and Mussels

Traditional Irish song

Eadd9 ... A/B

In Dub - lin's   fair   cit - y,   where   girls   are   so

C#m7 ... F#m9

pret - ty,   I   first   set   my   eyes   on   sweet   Mol - ly   Ma -

[2] **was, were, set, could**: past tenses of **is, are, set, can**
[3] **fishmonger**: fish dealer; **wheelbarrow**: a single-wheeled cart

B9sus4 — **Eadd9** — **Dadd9**

lone, As she wheeled her wheel - bar - row through streets broad and

CHORUS:

Amaj/C# — **Emaj/B** — **B9sus4**

nar - row, Cry - ing, "Cock-les and mus-sels, a - live, a - live

Eadd9 — **C#m9** — **F#m9**

oh! A - live, a - live oh, — a - live, a - live

B13 — **Amaj7** — **E/G#**

oh!" — Cry - ing, "Cock - les and mus - sels, a -

B9sus4 — **Eadd9**

live, a - live oh!"

𝄞 SONG LYRICS

1. In Dublin's fair city, where girls are so pretty,
   I first **set** my eyes on sweet Molly Malone,
   As she wheeled her wheelbarrow through streets broad and narrow,

   CHORUS: Crying, "Cockles and mussels, alive, alive oh!
                    Alive, alive oh, alive, alive oh!"
                    Crying, "Cockles and mussels, alive, alive oh!"

2. She **was** a fishmonger but sure **'twas** [4] no wonder
   For so **were** her father and mother before.
   And they each **wheeled** their barrow [5] through streets broad and narrow,   CHORUS

3. She **died** of a fever and no one **could** save her
   And that **was** the end of sweet Molly Malone.
   Her ghost wheels her barrow through streets broad and narrow,   CHORUS

LEARNING IDEAS

- *Vocabulary*

   Some lines from the song use the letter "e" many times. Fill in the rest of the letters for each line.

   1. _s_ _h_ e _w_ _h_ ee _l_ e _d_   _h_ e _r_   _w_ _h_ ee _l_ _b_ _a_ _r_ _r_ _o_ _w_
   2. " _ _ _ _ _ e _   _ _ _   _ _ _ _ e _ _ "
   3. _ _ e   _ _ e _   _ _   _   _ e _ e _
   4. _ _ e e _ _   _ _   _ _ ee _   _ _ _ _ _ _   _ _ _ _ _ e

- *Questions about the song*

   Read the Introduction to this song. Then write True, False, or ? if it doesn't say.

   1. Every country has its songs about pretty views. _____
   2. This is an old Chinese folk song. _____
   3. Molly Malone sells her fish in supermarkets. _____
   4. This song was written about 1550. _____
   5. Dublin, the capital city of Ireland, has many fish markets. _____

- *Questions for you*

   Answer the following questions with complete sentences.

   1. What is the capital of your country? _____

   _____

[4] **'twas**: contraction of **it was**
[5] **barrow**: abbreviation for **wheelbarrow**

2. What are your two favorite kinds of fish? _____

_____

3. When you were a child, did you ever go fishing? _____

_____

Where? _____

_____

What did you catch? _____

_____

- *Extra Learning*

Past Tense

Compose questions based on the following cue words. Then answer using information from the Song Lyrics.

1. Where / singer / first set eyes on / sweet Molly Malone?

   Q. _____

   _____

   A. _____

   _____

2. What / she / wheel through the streets?

   Q. _____

   _____

   A. _____

   _____

3. What / she / die of?

   Q. _____

   _____

   A. _____

   _____

4. Who / wheel / her barrow / now?

Q. _____

_____ ,

A. _____

_____

"As" + Clause

Choose clauses from the box to complete each sentence.

> As Edith studied the amoeba under her microscope   as he cleans his room
> as they reached the second peak   as her children crossed the street

1. Mrs. Ogawa watched _____ .

2. _____ , it changed shape.

3. Daniel sometimes listens to the radio _____ .

4. The hikers noticed the rain clouds _____ .

Now ask a partner to answer the following questions in complete sentences. Then let your partner ask you the same questions.

1. What do you do as you walk down the street?
2. Do you ever watch TV as you do your homework?
3. Make up two more questions.

Romantic Stories

Think of some romantic stories from your country. Choose two: one story that has a happy ending, and the other a sad ending. Form teams and tell them to your classmates. Let the other teams ask you more questions about the people in the stories you chose.

Pronunciation Practice

A "tongue twister" is a group of words that is difficult to pronounce. The second-to-last sentence in the Introduction to this song is a bit of a tongue twister: "Listen to the song to find out what she sings as she sells her fish." The following sentence is a real tongue twister: "She sells seashells by the seashore." Practice these sentences with some friends. See who can say them most quickly and most accurately.

WHEN I FIRST CAME TO THIS LAND

A street lined with shacks in the southern United States.

The Bettmann Archive

Moving to a new place and beginning a new life is exciting and difficult for anyone. For the first settlers in the "new land" of America, life was[1] a challenge. All the newcomers struggled. Many died. Others, to help themselves get through, made[1] jokes about the hardships and kept going[1].

This tune is from a famous melody known in many countries in Europe and the words are from an old Pennsylvania Dutch song. Oscar Brand, a twentieth-century folksinger, translated the words into English to express the troubles of an unlucky but optimistic farmer of a few centuries ago.

[1]**was, made, kept going**: past tense of **is, make, keep going** (phrasal verb)

KEY STRUCTURES

- **Past Tense, Irregular**   When I first **came**[2] + many others

- **Clauses**   **When I first came** + others

- **Expressions**   **"Break my back," "Run for your life"** + others

- **Reflexive Pronoun**   I got[2] **myself** a shack

COMMUNICATIVE OBJECTIVES

- to talk about easy and hard times

- to give descriptive names to people and places

When I First Came to This Land

English lyrics by OSCAR BRAND
Music traditional

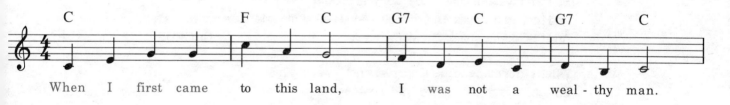

When I first came to this land, I was not a weal-thy man.

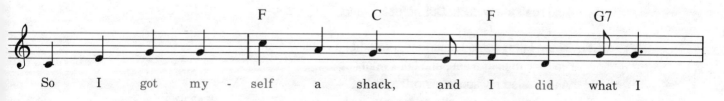

So I got my-self a shack, and I did what I

[2] **came, got**: past tense of **come, get**

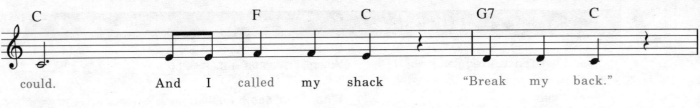

could. And I called my shack "Break my back."

CHORUS:

But the land was sweet and good,___ and I did what I could.

 SONG LYRICS

1. **When I first came** to this land, I **was** not a wealthy man.
   So I **got myself** a shack, and I **did**[3] what I **could**[3].
   And I **called** my shack "**Break my back.**"

   CHORUS: But the land **was** sweet and good, and I **did** what I **could**.

2. **When I first came** to this land, I **was** not a wealthy man.
   So I **got myself** a wife, and I **did** what I **could**.
   And I **called** my wife "**Run for your life!**"
   And I **called** my shack "**Break my back.**"   CHORUS

3. **When I first came** to this land, I **was** not a wealthy man.
   So I **got myself** a duck, and I **did** what I **could**.
   And I **called** my duck "**Out of luck.**" And I **called** my wife "**Run for your life!**"
   And I **called** my shack "**Break my back.**"   CHORUS

4. **When I first came** to this land, I **was** not a wealthy man.
   So I **got myself** a cow, and I **did** what I **could**.
   And I **called** my cow "**No milk now.**"
   And I **called** my duck "**Out of luck.**"—etc.   CHORUS

5. **When I first came** to this land, I **was** not a wealthy man.
   So I **got myself** a son, and I **did** what I **could**.
   And I **called** my son "**My work's done.**"
   And I **called** my cow "**No milk now.**"—etc.   CHORUS

[3]**did, could**: past tense of **do, can**

LEARNING IDEAS

- *Vocabulary*

  In this song, which words are new for you? Write them down. Can you use them in sentences?

- *Questions about the song*

  Put these words from the song in correct order. Use quotation marks and punctuation as needed.

  1. my Break called my I back And shack

     _____

  2. what cow I did So could myself and I a got I

     _____

  3. land I wealthy first to not this I a When man came was

     _____

- *Questions for you*

  Think about a time when you first came to a new place, whether it was a neighborhood, a school, a city, or a country.

  1. What was something difficult that happened to you? _____

     _____

     _____

  2. What was something amusing? _____

     _____

     _____

  Write down your remembrances. Then tell them to your class. Let your classmates ask you questions.

- *Extra Learning*

  Reflexive Pronouns
  Use reflexive pronouns from the box to complete the following sentences. Begin all your answers with "No." In some sentences you may use the prepositions **"by," "for,"** or **"to."**

1. Did the farmer get a duck for his neighbor?

   No, *he got himself a duck.*

2. Did Dolores walk to the drugstore with her cousin?

3. Do you usually do your homework with friends?

4. I hear some mumbling. Is Victor talking to you?

5. Do you and your brother live with your parents?

6. Do Jessica and Marco like to go to the movies with a bunch of people?

Descriptive Names

The farmer in this song makes up amusing expressions to describe the members of his family, his animals, and his house. Can you match the names in the box with the descriptions given below?

Australia	China	U. S. Government	Egypt
Japan	New York City	Paris	Peru
Rome	Saudi Arabia	large clock in London	dog

1. The Big Apple *New York City*

2. The City of Lovers

3. A man's best friend

4. Country of the Great Wall

5. Home of the Llama

6. Big Ben

7. Land of Oil

8. Uncle Sam

9. Land of the Pyramids

10. The City of Fountains

11. The Land Down Under

12 Land of the Rising Sun

Now use your imagination to make up descriptive names for the following:

1. your hometown _____

_____

2. your favorite restaurant _____

_____

3. your best friend _____

_____

4. your favorite vacation place _____

_____

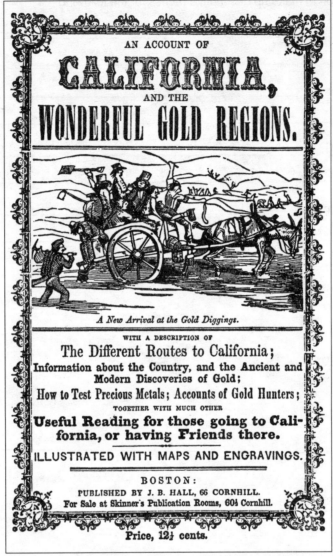

Cover from a book published about the
California Gold Rush of the 1850s.

The Bettmann Archive

This song became[1] popular when people rushed to California to find gold in 1849, but the melody is probably much older. Toward the end of the 19th century, "Clementine" was a favorite in the city of San Francisco. Then college and community groups picked it up. Now people in Chile, China, and the Czech Republic know about this famous woman named Clementine. Clementine was the daughter of an old miner who went out to California during the Gold Rush. In later years, university singers added on the last verse.

[1] **became:** past tense of **become**

KEY STRUCTURES

- **Past tense**

  Verb "to be"   She **was** light, her shoes **were** number nine

  Regular   **stubbed** her toe + others

  Irregular   She **drove**[2] ducklings + many others

- **"How" as emphasis**   **How** I missed her!

- **Past Participle as Adjective**   You are **lost**[3] and **gone**[3] forever.

- **Review of Clauses, Gerunds as Adjectives, Reductions**

COMMUNICATIVE OBJECTIVES

- to talk about things you or someone else ought to do
- to describe people
- to talk about events

Clementine

Traditional song

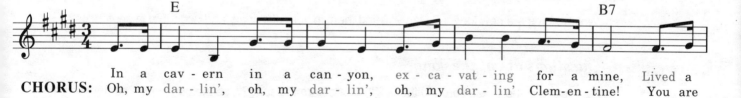

In a cav-ern in a can-yon, ex-ca-vat-ing for a mine, Lived a

CHORUS: Oh, my dar-lin', oh, my dar-lin', oh, my dar-lin' Clem-en-tine! You are

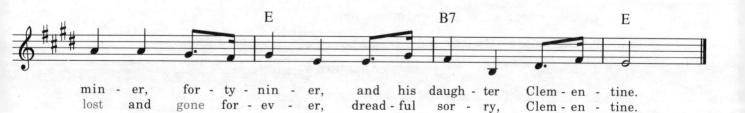

min-er, for-ty-nin-er, and his daugh-ter Clem-en-tine.

lost and gone for-ev-er, dread-ful sor-ry, Clem-en-tine.

[2]**drove**: past tense of **drive**
[3]**lost, gone**: past participles of **lose, go**

SONG LYRICS

1. In a cavern in a canyon, **excavating** for a mine,
   Lived a miner, forty-niner[4], and his daughter Clementine.

   CHORUS: Oh, my **darlin'**, oh, my **darlin'**, oh, my **darlin'** Clementine!
               You are **lost** and **gone** forever, dreadful[5] sorry, Clementine.

2. She **was** light and like a fairy and her shoes **were** number nine.
   Herring boxes without topses[5] **were** sandals for Clementine.   CHORUS

3. She **drove** ducklings to the water every morning just at nine,
   Stubbed her toe against a splinter, **fell**[6] into the foaming brine.   CHORUS

4. Ruby lips above the water **blowing** bubbles soft and fine,
   But, alas,[7] I **was** no swimmer so I **lost**[6] my Clementine.   CHORUS

5. Then the miner, forty-niner, soon **began**[6] to peak and pine,[7]
   Thought[6] he ought to join his daughter. Now he's with his Clementine.   CHORUS

6. **How** I **missed** her, **how** I **missed** her, **how** I **missed** my Clementine!
   Until I **kissed** her baby sister and **forgot**[6] my Clementine.   CHORUS

LEARNING IDEAS

- *Vocabulary*

  Which words are new for you? Can you find them in your dictionary and use them in sentences?

- *Questions about the song*

  Can you fill in the spaces around these "S" words from the song? Use the cues in the sentences below to help you. Then insert the words into the proper sentences.

  1. Clementine's s __ __ __s were size nine.

  2. Every morning she drove d __ __ __ __ __ __ __ s to the water.

  3 & 4. She s __ __ __ __ __ __ her toe against a s __ __ __ __ __ __ __ __.

  5 & 6. A __ __ s, Clementine's father wasn't a good s __ __ __ __ __ __ __ !

---

[4] **forty-niner**: a person who was in the Gold Rush of 1849
[5] **dreadful, topses**: poetic license for the purpose of adding rhythm and rhyme; in correct English, **dreadfully** and **tops**
[6] **fell, lost, began, thought, forgot**: past tense of **fall, lose, begin, think, forget**
[7] **alas**: an expression of sadness and regret; **peak and pine**: feel very sad

- *Questions for you*

    1. When you were a kid, did you usually wear shoes or sandals in the summertime?

        _____

        Tell when and where you wore[8] each.   _____

        _____

    2. Did you ever go barefoot?   _____

        _____

    3. About how many times a week did you stub your toe?   _____

        _____

    Now practice asking and answering these questions with a partner.

- *Extra Learning*

    Past Participle as Adjective

    Match the following sentences with the sentences in the box below.

    1. Clementine will never come back again.   _____

    2. Her father misses her very much.   _____

    3. The miner dug[9] all the mines he needed to.   _____

    4. Julio Iglesias is famous in many countries.   _____

    5. Thousands of people walk to the top of Machu Picchu every year.   _____

He is extremely well-known.	**His work is all done.**	**He feels lost.**
That path is very well-worn.	**She is gone forever.**	

    Now compose your own sentences using **done**, **gone**, **lost**, and **well-known**.

    _____

    _____

    _____

    _____

[8] **wore**: past tense of **wear**
[9] **dug**: past tense of **dig**

"How" as emphasis

Use your imagination to complete these sentences.

1. How / lost / little girl _____

2. How / frightened / little dog _____

3. beautiful / sky _____

4. surprised / my teacher _____

5. embarrassed / I _____

Now write two of your own sentences using "How."

_____

_____

Ought to

Olga plans to enter a triathlon event three months from now. She'll need to swim 10 kilometers, bike ride 30 miles, and swim 5 miles. What do you think Olga ought to do to get in good shape? Let someone play the part of Olga, and you tell her three things she ought to do in each of the following areas:

1. Diet _____

   _____

   _____

2. Physical Exercise _____

   _____

   _____

3. Mental Concentration _____

   _____

   _____

COMPOSITION

Compose your own TV interview.

Imagine that you just got back[1] from a space trip to Saturn. Maribel Soares, the chief interviewer for the TV show "Science and Travel," wants you to appear on her show. She will want to know what you ate[1], what you wore[1], how long you were away, who went[1] with you, what you discovered, how you felt[1], what the most difficult part of the journey was, what the most surprising discovery was, and many other things. Write the interviewer's questions and your answers.

Maribel: _____

You: _____

Maribel: _____

You: _____

Maribel: _____

You: _____

Maribel: _____

You: _____

Maribel: _____

You: _____

Maribel: _____

You: _____

Now act out the TV interview. Have a producer, lighting and camera director, sets manager, etc.

QUESTIONS

Think about when you first began to study English. Now answer the questions below in complete sentences.

1. When did you first understand something you heard?

   _____

   Where were you? _____

2. What did you understand?

   _____

3. Which did you find harder, spelling or pronouncing words in English?

   _____

Now ask a partner these questions. Then read your answers to your partner. Compare your responses.

---

[1] **got back, ate, wore, went, felt:** past tense of **get back** (phrasal verb), **eat, wear, go, feel**

- **EXAGGERATIONS**

Clementine was light and like a fairy, yet she was so clumsy that she tripped over a splinter! Can you compose exaggerated sentences to go with the following?

1. Queen Esmerelda was incredibly gorgeous.

_____

2. Jimmy Johnson was an extremely good swimmer.

_____

3. The rush-hour train was so empty that

_____

4. Last winter it was so cold (that)

_____

5. Last night I was so tired that

_____

- **CLAUSES AND PAST TENSE**

Find the missing part of each sentence from the box. Sometimes more than one ending is possible.

so he got himself a cold drink.	"Wow, this city is too fast for me!"
what he could to help her.	he tried to move as fast as he could.
an old lady rushed by him and tripped on the curb.	
he was amazed to see so many people moving so quickly.	

1. Michael did _____

2. One day when he came out of the subway station, _____

_____

3. He said to himself, _____

4. When Michael arrived in New York, _____

_____

5. Then he needed to relax _____

6. To be like the New Yorkers, _____

Now put the sentences in the correct order to tell a story. Find the best ending for the story.

_____

_____

LEMON TREE

Trini Lopez, Mexican-American singer, in the studio.

UPI/Bettmann

Why does a blossom as beautiful and fragrant as the lemon have a fruit that tastes so sour? Or, in other words, are first impressions sometimes deceiving?

In this song, the composer Will Holt likens[1] the lemon tree to young love, which is beautiful but sometimes turns sour. He lets the father give advice to his son about young love. Have you ever received[2] advice like this?

The folk trio of Peter, Paul and Mary had[3] their first big hit with this song. Then the Mexican-American vocalist Trini Lopez helped many other people learn about the "Lemon Tree."

[1] **likens** = compares
[2] **Have you ever received**: present perfect tense, interrogative
[3] **had**: past tense of **have**

59

KEY STRUCTURES

- **Past Tense**

  Verb "to be"   When I **was** just a little boy

  Regular   When she **smiled** + others

  Irregular   my father **said**[4] to me + others

- **Phrasal Verbs**   She **took**[4] **away** the sun, she **left**[4] **behind**

- **Comparative Adjectives**   a **sadder** man but **wiser** now

- **Superlative Adverb**   It's [the] **most** important

- **Review of Imperative, Present Tense, Adverbs, Clauses, Participle as Adjective, Possessive, Quotations**

COMMUNICATIVE OBJECTIVES

- to talk about what advice your parents gave you when you were young

- to tell what advice you imagine you will give to your children

Lemon Tree

Words and Music by WILL HOLT

When   I   was   just   a   lit - tle   boy,—   my   fa - ther   said   to   me,—

---

[4] **said, took, left**: past tense of **say, take, leave** (**leave behind** = phrasal verb)

"Come here and learn a les-son from the love-ly lem-on tree.

My son it's most im-por-tant," my fa-ther said to me,

"To put your faith in what you feel and not in what you see."

CHORUS:

Lem-on tree, ve-ry pret-ty, and the lem-on flow-er is

sweet, but the fruit of the poor lem-on is im-poss-i-ble to eat.

Lem-on Tree ve-ry pret-ty, and the lem-on flow-er is

sweet, but the fruit of the poor lem-on is im-poss-i-ble to eat.

SONG LYRICS

1. When I **was** just a little boy, my father **said** to me,
    "**Come** here and **learn** a lesson from the lovely lemon tree.
    My son, it's **most** important," my father **said** to me,
    "To put your faith in what you feel and not in what you see."

say – said
chorus

    CHORUS: Lemon tree, very pretty, and the lemon flower is sweet.
                But the fruit of the poor lemon is impossible to eat.

                                                    REPEAT CHORUS

2. Beneath the lemon tree one day, my love and I **did lie**[5],
    A girl so sweet that when she **smiled** the sun **rose**[5] in the sky.
    We **passed** the summer **lost**[5] in love beneath the lemon tree.   CHORUS
    The music of her laughter **hid**[5] my father's words from me.

3. One day she **left** without a word. She **took**[5] **away** the sun.
    And in the dark she **left behind**, I **knew**[5] what she had **done**[6].
    She **left** me for another: it's a common tale but true.
    A **sadder** man **but wiser** now I sing these words to you: CHORUS

4. (spoken) Ha, ha, ha! Now you know, young man, about the little lemon tree.
    It's very sweet and it's very pretty, but you know it's impossible to eat.
    Now, one summer you may pass your time away sitting under that very lemon tree, young man.
    But don't let your heart get in the way of your mind. Ha, ha, ha, ha!
    Just be happy, young man. Just be happy.

LEARNING IDEAS

*   *Vocabulary*
    Write down any new words and use them in sentences.

*   *Questions about the song*

    Listen to the song without looking at the words. Can you hear the words needed to complete the lines below?

    1. The girl was so _____ that when she _____ the _____ rose in

       the _____ .

    2. "Come _____ and _____ a lesson from the _____ _____ _____."

[5]**did, rose, lost, hid, took, knew**: past tense of **do, rise, lose, hide, take** (**take away** = phrasal verb), **know. Did lie: did** adds emphasis; past tense of **lie** = **lay**.
[6]**had done**: past perfect of **do**. See Level Four for more examples.

62

3. We passed _____ _____ lost _____ _____ .

4. _____ left me _____ _____ .

- ## Questions for you

  1. What advice did your father give to you regarding members of the opposite sex? _____

     _____

     _____

  2. What advice did your mother give? _____

     _____

     _____

  3. Did your parents give the same advice or different advice to their sons and their daughters?

     Explain. _____

     _____

  4. Do you agree that the fruit of the lemon tree is impossible to eat? Explain. _____

     _____

     _____

  5. Now ask a partner these same questions. How do your partner's responses compare with yours?

     _____

     _____

- ## Extra Learning

  ### Comparatives and Superlatives

  Discuss the following questions with a friend. Give reasons for your answers.

  1. Who do you think is a better all-around athlete: Pelé or Michael Jordan? _____

     _____

     _____

  2. Who do you think is a better performer and musician: Gloria Estefan or Madonna? _____

     _____

     _____

3. Who do you think is sadder: a person with no money or a person with no friends? _____

_____

_____

4. What do you think is the most important thing for success in life? _____

_____

_____

Phrasal (two-word) Verbs and Giving Advice

Imagine that you are the parent of 15-year-old twins, a boy and a girl. The twins are away from home for the first time, studying at a summer institute in another country. Write a letter giving them advice. If possible, use these phrasal verbs in your letter: **go through, grow up, leave behind, let in, look back, take away, take care.**

Betty Hutton shows off as Annie in "Annie Get Your Gun."   *The Bettmann Archive*

Do you have a friend who always says he can do something better than you? If you speak English, he says he can speak it better than you. If you run a race, he says he can run it faster. In this song, two friends boast about what they can do. When the girl claims "I can do anything better than you," the guy replies, "No, you can't."

Irving Berlin, one of America's greatest songwriters, wrote this song for the musical "Annie Get Your Gun." Irving was born in Temun, Russia and came[1] to New York as a child. He went[1] to school only two years and taught[1] himself music. When he died in 1989 at the age of 101, people gathered in the street outside his house to honor his passing by singing his songs.

[1] **came, went, taught**: past tense of **come, go, teach**

KEY STRUCTURES

- **Past, Irregular**   where you **went**, what I **thought**[2] + others

- **Comparatives**   **better than you, cheaper** + many others

- **Neither**   **Neither** can I!

- **Review of Present Tense, Modal (can), Pronouns**

COMMUNICATIVE OBJECTIVES

- to express ability

- to challenge someone else to do something

- to make comparisons

Anything You Can Do

Words and music by IRVING BERLIN

INTRODUCTION:

I'm su - pe - ri - or; you're in - fe - ri - or. I'm the big at - trac-tion;

you're the small.___ I'm the ma - jor one; you're the mi - nor one.

I can beat you shoot - in' — that's not all.___

[2] **thought**: past tense of **think**

SONG LYRICS

INTRODUCTION:

I'm superior; you're inferior. I'm the big attraction; you're the small.
I'm the major one; you're the minor one. I can beat you shootin'—that's not all.

1. Anything you **can** do, I **can** do **better**. I **can** do anything **better than you**.
   No you **can't**.   Yes I **can**.   REPEAT
   No you **can't**.   Yes I **can**.   Yes I **can**.

2. Anything you **can** be, I **can** be **greater**. **Sooner** or **later**, I'm **greater than you**.
   No you're not.   Yes I am.   REPEAT
   No you're not.   Yes I am.   Yes I am.

   > BRIDGE: I **can** shoot a partridge with a single cartridge.
   > I **can** get a sparrow with a bow and arrow.
   > I **can** do most[3] anything. **Can** you bake a pie?
   > No. **Neither can** I.

3. Anything you **can** sing I **can** sing **louder**[4]. I **can** sing anything **louder than you**.
   No you **can't**—etc.

4. Anything you **can** buy, I **can** buy **cheaper**[4]. I **can** buy anything **cheaper than you**.
   Fifty cents.   Forty cents.   Thirty cents.   Twenty cents.
   No you **can't**.   Yes I **can**.   Yes I **can**.

5. Anything you **can** dig, I **can** dig **deeper**[4]. I **can** dig anything **deeper than you**.
   Thirty feet.   Forty feet.   Fifty feet.   Sixty feet.
   No you **can't**.   Yes I **can**.   Yes I **can**.

   > BRIDGE: I **can** drink my liquor **faster than a flicker**.
   > I **can** do it **quicker** and get even **sicker**.
   > I **can** live on bread and cheese. And only on that?
   > Yes. So can a rat!

6. Any note you **can** reach, I **can** go **higher**. I **can** sing anything **higher than you**.
   No you **can't**—etc.

---

[3] **most**: reduced from **almost**
[4] **louder, cheaper, deeper**: used often in spoken English. It is more proper to say, **I can buy anything more cheaply, dig more deeply**, etc.

7. Anyone you **can** lick[5], I **can** lick **faster**. I **can** lick anyone **faster than you**.

   With your fist.   With my feet.   With your feet.   With an axe.

   No you **can't**.   Yes I **can**.   Yes I **can**.

8. Any school where you **went**, I **could**[6] be master. I **could** be master **much faster than you**.

   Can you spell?   No I **can't**.   **Can** you add?   No I can't.

   Can you teach?   Yes I **can**.   Yes I **can**.

             BRIDGE: I **could** be a racer, quite a steeplechaser.

                           I **can** jump a hurdle even with my girdle.

                           I **can** open any safe.   Without being caught[7]?

                           Yeah[8].   That's what I **thought**!

9. Any note you **can** hold I can hold **longer**. I **can** hold any note **longer than you**.

   No you **can't**—etc.

LEARNING IDEAS

- *Vocabulary*

   Make up a funny story using these words: **bow and arrow, bread and cheese, flicker, liquor, master, sparrow.**

- *Questions about the song*

   Can you unscramble these words from the song? Write them down and then write their opposites.

   1.   erriopus   s *uperior*   *inferior*

   2.   nooers   s_____   _____

   3.   repceah   c_____   _____

   4.   tsrfea   f_____   _____

   5.   rhhegi   h_____   _____

- *Questions for you*

   Answer in complete sentences.

   1.   Which is heavier: an elephant or a rhinoceros? _____

   _____

   2.   Which car is cheaper: a Mercedes or a Ford? _____

   _____

---

[5] **lick**: to get the better of; to overcome
[6] **could**: modal expressing possibility. See Level Five for more examples.
[7] **being caught**: gerund and past participle of **catch**
[8] **yeah**: colloquial for **yes**

3. Who do you think sings better: Rubén Blades or Luis Miguel? _____

_____

4. Which is higher: Mt. Everest or the Empire State Building? _____

_____

5. Now compose two of your own questions and ask someone to make the comparisons.

•   *Extra Learning*

Neither, Either, Both

Look at the chart below to see who can do what. Then write complete answers to the questions using
both, either, neither, only, or **too** when suitable.

Name	play soccer	swim 5 miles	lift 200 pounds	speak Japanese	play guitar
Alex		✔	✔		✔
Suzie	✔	✔		✔	✔
Vittorio	✔	✔			✔
you					

1. Does either Vittorio or Suzie play guitar? _____

_____

2. Does Alex play guitar? _____

_____

3. Does Alex speak Japanese? _____

_____

4. Does Vittorio speak Japanese? _____

_____

5. Do you speak Japanese? _____

   _____

6. Who can lift 200 pounds? _____

   _____

A. Make up some of your own questions about the people above. Ask a partner.
B. Substitute the names in the chart with names of your classmates and do a survey.
C. Challenge a partner. Choose three things you think you can do better than your partner. Then let your partner pick three different things. Ask two other people to be judges. Then act out each challenge and let the judges make a chart and mark down who does what better.

OH, SUSANNA!

A banjo player and admirer from a painting by Eastman Johnson.

The Bettmann Archive

Stephen Foster, the composer of this song, was born in Kentucky in 1826. He wrote[1] many songs about plantation life as he saw[1] it. His words and melodies give us glimpses of southern USA in the late 1800s. Foster's songs were popularized[2] by banjo-playing singers who traveled from town to town.

Stephen Foster's songs have been known[2] as American classics for over a century. Now people in Korea, Poland and many other countries know and love "Oh, Susanna!," "Jeanie with the Light Brown Hair," and other songs by Foster.

---

[1] **wrote, saw:** past tense of **write, see**
[2] **were popularized:** past tense, passive voice, **were made popular; have been known:** present perfect tense, passive voice. See Level Four for more examples.

KEY STRUCTURES

- **Past, Irregular**   I **froze**[3] to death + many others

- **Quotation**   I **said**[3] to her, **"I'm coming, girl."**

- **"So" + Adjective**   The sun **so hot** (that) I froze to death

- **Review of Imperative, Present, Present Continuous and Future Tenses, Clauses, Gerund as Adjective**

COMMUNICATIVE OBJECTIVES

- to recognize nonsensical (just-for-fun) combinations and create your own

- to talk about famous composers from your country

Oh, Susanna!

Words and Music by STEPHEN FOSTER

I come from Al - a - bam - a with my ban - jo on my knee. I'm
It rained all night the day I left; the wea - ther was so dry. The

going to Louis - i - a - na my true loved one to see.
sun so hot I froze to death. Su - san - na, don't you cry.

CHORUS:

Oh, Su - san - na! Oh, don't you cry for me! I

come from Al - a - bam - a with my ban - jo on my knee.

[3] **froze, said:** past tense of **freeze, say**

1. I **come** from Alabama with my banjo on my knee.
   I'm **going** to Louisiana my true loved one to see.
   It **rained** all night the day I **left**[4]; the weather **was**[4] so dry,
   The sun **so hot** I froze to death. Susanna, **don't you cry!**

   > CHORUS: Oh, Susanna! Oh, **don't you cry for me!**
   >   I **come** from Alabama with my banjo on my knee.

2. I **had**[4] a dream the other night when everything was still.
   I **thought**[4] I **saw**[4] Susanna comin' down the hill.
   A buckwheat cake **was** in her mouth. A tear was in her eye.
   I said to her, "I'm **comin', girl. Susanna, don't you cry!**"   CHORUS

3. Oh, I soon **will be** in New Orleans and then I'**ll look** around.
   And when I find Susanna, I'**ll fall** upon the ground.
   But if I do not find her, then I **will** surely **die.**
   And when I'm dead and buried, Susanna, don't you cry!   CHORUS

LEARNING IDEAS

- *Vocabulary*

  Can you find the two nonsensical combinations in verse 1? Write them down.

  _____

  _____

- *Questions about the song*

  Read the Introduction and the Song Lyrics. Circle T (True), F (False), or ?(Not Known)
  beside each of the following statements. If the statement is false, circle the error and write in the
  correction.

  1. Stephen Foster was born in Colorado in 1926.   T F ?

  _____

  2. Stephen played piano and violin when he was young.   T F ?

  _____

  3. Guitar-playing singers popularized his songs.   T F ?

  _____

[4]left, was, had, thought, saw: past tense of **leave, is, has, think, see**

74

4. People in Korea and Poland know "Oh, Susanna!" T F ?

_____

5. The singer thought he saw Susanna coming down the street. T F ?

_____

6. The singer finally found Susanna in New Orleans. T F ?

_____

- ## Questions for you

1. Who are two of the most famous composers from your country? _____

_____

2. What are your favorite songs by these composers? _____

_____

3. Tell why you like each song. _____

_____

- ## Extra Learning

Quotations

Imagine that the singer (let's call him Johnny) of this song traveled for 25 years looking for Susanna. Then one sunny morning, Johnny walked into a diner and saw a woman who looked exactly like Susanna. Make up a conversation between the two of them using quotations.

Johnny said, " _Oh, Susanna! It's you!_ _____ "

The **woman** replied, " _____ ."

Then **Johnny** said, " _____ "

The **woman** answered, " _____ ."

Then **Johnny** _____

The **woman** _____

Johnny _____

The **woman** _____

"So" + (that +) Adjective in Nonsensical Combinations

"The sun so hot (that) I froze to death" is an example of an absurd, just-for-fun description. Can you create nonsensical endings for the following phrases? It is correct to say the sentences with or without "that."

1. The river was so deep that _____

2. My cup of coffee was so cold that _____

3. That boy is so ugly _____

Now create some of your own nonsensical combinations and share them with a partner.

- *Past Tense Verbs*

    1. Listen to the song. Write down at least five past tense verbs that you hear.

    _____   _____

    _____   _____

    _____   _____

    2. Use three of the five verbs you just chose to compose your own sentences, both in the present and past tenses.

    _____   _____
    (verb 1)   (present tense)

    _____
    (past tense)

    _____   _____
    (verb 2)   (present tense)

    _____
    (past tense)

    _____   _____
    (verb 3)   (present tense)

    _____
    (past tense)

Linda Ronstadt sings a Mexican song in concert with a mariachi band.   *Reuters/Bettmann*

Linda Ronstadt was born in Tucson, Arizona, and was raised[2] in a family of avid musicians. As a child she heard big-band music, country music, Mexican ballads, and rock-and-roll. Linda mastered all of these styles and then added soul, folk, and opera to her singing repertoire.

In her latest albums and CDs,[3] Linda returns to her Mexican-American roots to sing songs she learned from her father. Two of these songs, "Frenesí" and "Perfidia," were written[2] by the famous Mexican composer, Alberto Domínguez.

---

[1] **Frenesí:** Spanish for **frenzy** or **passion**
[2] **was raised, were written:** past tense, passive voice of **raise, write**
[3] **CDs:** abbreviation for **compact disks**

KEY STRUCTURES

- **Past tense**

Verb "to be"	While I **was**[4] there; her eyes **were**[4] soft
Regular	I **wandered** down into old Mexico + others
Irregular	I **felt**[4] romance ev'rywhere + many others
Modal	I **could**[4] say, "Frenesí"

- **"So" as Conjunction**   **So** how was I to resist?

- **Review of Adverbs, Clauses, Comparisons, Quotations**

COMMUNICATIVE OBJECTIVES

- to talk about celebrations, fiestas, parties

- to discuss what you knew and didn't know two years ago and ten years ago

Frenesí

Music by ALBERTO DOMINGUEZ
English Words by RAY CHARLES & S.K. RUSSEL

INTRODUCTION:

[4] **was, were, felt, could**: past tense of **is, are, feel, can**

SONG LYRICS

INTRODUCTION:
Sometime ago I **wander'd** down into old Mexico.
While I **was** there, I **felt** romance ev'rywhere.
Moon was shining[5] bright[6], and I **could** hear laughing voices in the night;
Ev'ryone **was** gay. This **was** the start of their holiday.

1. It **was** fiesta[7] down in Mexico and **so** I **stopped** a while to see the show.
    I **knew**[8] that "Frenesí" **meant**[8] **"Please, love me."**
    And I **could** say **"Frenesí."**

2. A lovely señorita[9] **caught**[8] my eye. I **stood**[8] enchanted as she **wander'd** by,
    And never knowing that it **came**[8] from me, I **gently sighed "Frenesí."**

        BRIDGE: She **stopped** and **raised** her eyes to mine.
                   Her lips just **pleaded** to be kissed.
                   Her eyes **were** soft as candleshine, **so** how **was** I to resist?

3. And now without a heart to call my own, **a greater** happiness I've never known[10]
    Because her kisses are for me alone. Who wouldn't[11] say **"Frenesí?"**

                                    INSTRUMENTAL + BRIDGE + verse 3

LEARNING IDEAS

*   *Vocabulary*

    Linda Ronstadt sings many kinds of music. In the puzzle on the next page, can you circle seven
    types of music she sings? Clue: three words go → and four go ↓.

---

[5] **was shining**: past continuous tense. See Level Four for more examples.
[6] **bright**: poetic license to rhyme with **night**. In correct English, the moon was shining **brightly**.
[7] **fiesta**: Spanish for **party** or **celebration**
[8] **knew, meant, caught, stood, came**: past tense of **know, mean, catch, stand, come**
[9] **señorita**: Spanish for **young woman**
[10] **I've never known**: present perfect tense. See Level Four for more examples.
[11] **wouldn't**: modal, **would not**

W	E	S	T	B	A	L	L	A	D	S	O	F
A	S	M	B	I	E	P	U	D	S	V	K	L
R	S	B	M	G	J	W	T	G	E	S	Y	O
R	O	C	K	–	A	N	D	–	R	O	L	L
L	U	O	T	B	W	A	S	X	H	P	C	P
W	L	U	Y	A	I	T	D	B	E	E	Q	Z
E	A	N	W	N	S	B	O	C	O	R	Y	B
T	S	T	N	D	F	F	O	L	K	A	E	J
W	M	R	P	L	E	H	R	E	T	S	O	P
A	S	Y	F	R	E	N	E	S	I	T	A	R

- ## Questions about the song

Listen to the song. Find the errors in the sentences below and circle them. Then write each sentence correctly. Be careful! Some of the sentences have many errors.

1. Somewhere ago you wandered up into new Morocco. _____

_____

_____

2. I stopped ten minutes to watch the movie. _____

_____

_____

3. I know that "Frenesí" means "Please, move your car." _____

_____

_____

4. An ugly señorita caught my ear. _____

_____

_____

- ## *Questions for you*

  Answer the following questions with complete sentences.

  1. Ten years ago, how well could you dance? _____

  _____

  2. Two years ago, how much English did you speak? _____

  _____

  3. One year ago, about how many songs in English did you know? _____

  _____

  4. How many songs in English do you know now? _____

  _____

  5. Which ones are your favorites? _____

  _____

- ## *Extra Learning*

  ### "So" as Conjunction + Past Tense

  Use the phrases in the box to finish each sentence.

so he caught a cold.	so I started it for him.
so I taught her.	so I offered him a sandwich.

  1. Marisol didn't know how to dance to rock-and-roll music, _____

  _____

  2. Mr. Yamaguchi couldn't start his car, _____

  _____

3. Peter looked hungry, _____

_____

4. He didn't wear a jacket on that freezing day, _____

_____

Now make up an alternate ending for each of the sentences above. Compare your answers with someone else's.

• *Composition*

Imagine that you are the grand winner of a contest sponsored by MEX-TOUR TRAVELS. As the top winner, you are entitled to a one-week vacation for yourself and a friend in one of the following places:

Chichen-Itza and other Mayan ruins in the Yucatan Peninsula
Mexico City and its environs
Acapulco or Cancún and surrounding beaches
Cuernavaca and San Luis Potosí

Choose your vacation site. Now imagine that you are there with a friend. Write a postcard to your folks back home telling them where you went, what you did, who you met, what you bought, etc. in your first day and night there.

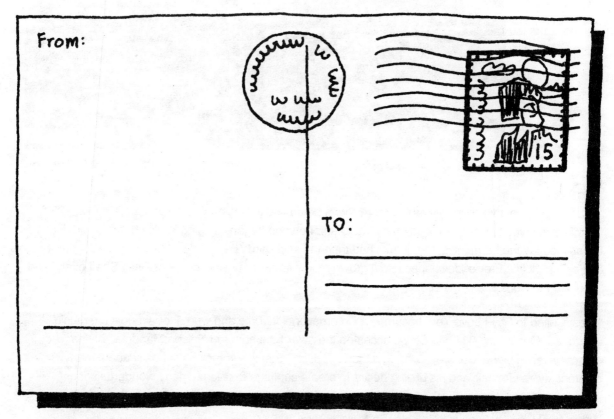

Stevie Wonder performs at the Grammy Awards.   *UPI/Bettmann*

The author of this song, Steveland Morris, was born blind in Saginaw, Michigan, on May 13, 1950. Little Stevie loved to listen to songs on the radio and he soon began[1] singing in his church choir. He taught[1] himself to play the harmonica, the drums, and then the keyboard. By age 13, "Little Stevie Wonder" had his first big hit. "Little Stevie" developed into a grown man with such musical gems as "Isn't She Lovely" and "You Are the Sunshine of My Life."

"I Just Called to Say I Love You" became[1] an international favorite and won[1] Hollywood's top music award, an "Oscar," in 1984. As Stevie accepted the award, he honored Nelson Mandela, the leader of the African National Congress who was then in prison. Stevie's voracious curiosity about many different styles of music and his driving desire to create continue to give us many wonderful songs.

[1]**began, taught, became, won:** past tense of **begin, teach, become, win**

KEY STRUCTURES

- **Past Tense**

  Regular   I just **called**

  Modal   no three words **could**[2] ever **do**

- **Hyphenated Adjective**   **choc'late-covered**[3] candy hearts

- **Infinitive of Purpose**   I just called **to say** I love you

- **Review of Present Tense, Possessives**

COMMUNICATIVE OBJECTIVES

- to practice telephone calls to friends and to business places

- to talk about holidays, seasons, and astrological signs

I Just Called To Say I Love You

Words and music by STEVIE WONDER

1. No New Year's Day   to cel - e - brate;
2.   rain;   no flow - ers bloom;

no choc - 'late - cov - ered can - dy hearts___ to give___ a - way.
no wed - ding Sat - ur - day___ with - in___ the month___ of June.

[2]**could**: past tense of **can**
[3]**choc'late-covered**: reduction **of chocolate-covered**

Gm7 C Dm7

— to say___ I love_____ you.___ And I mean

Gm7 C7sus C7 F Bb/C *D.S. al fine*
fine

— it from_ the bot - tom of___ my___ heart. 3. No sum - mer's

SONG LYRICS

1. No **New Year's Day** to celebrate; no **choc'late-covered**[3] candy hearts to give away.
No first of **spring**[4]; no song to sing. In fact here's just another ordinary day.

2. No April rain; no flowers bloom; no wedding Saturday within the month of June.
But what it is is something true made up of these three words that I must[5] say to you.

CHORUS: I just **called to say** I love you
                I just **called to say** how much I care.
                I just **called to say** I love you.
                And I mean it from the bottom of my heart.

3. No **summer's high**; no warm July; no harvest moon to light one tender August night.
No **autumn** breeze; no falling leaves; not even time for birds to fly to southern skies.

4. No **Libra** sun; no **Halloween**[6]; no giving thanks to all the **Christmas** joy you bring.
But what it is, though old so new, to fill your heart like no three words **could** ever do.

CHORUS

---

[3]**choc'late-covered:** reduction of **chocolate-covered**
[4]**spring:** in English, the seasons may be capitalized or not. **Spring** and **spring** are both correct.
[5]**must:** modal meaning **have to**. See Level Five for more examples.
[6]**Halloween:** All Hallows Evening, October 31, the evening before All Saints' Day. Children often dress up as ghosts and other characters and go door-to-door asking for candy.

LEARNING IDEAS

- *Vocabulary*

  Stevie Wonder mentions three specific holidays in this song. Can you find each one? Write the name, its date, and its significance on the lines below.

  1. _____

  2. _____

  3. _____

- *Questions about the song*

  1. Stevie specifically names three of the four seasons. Write the phrases containing these seasons.

     _____

     _____

     _____

     Which season doesn't he name? _____

  2. Four months of the year appear in the song. Write the corresponding phrases for each.

     _____

     _____

     _____

     _____

  3. Stevie gives information about the eight other months. Can you name four of them and identify them by clues Stevie gives? _____

     _____

     _____

     _____

- *Questions for you*

  1. In the United States, rain and early-blooming flowers are associated with April. In your country, what are two things associated with April? _____

     _____

     _____

  2. In what month do most people marry in your country? _____

On what day of the week? _____

At what time of the day? _____

What do they wear? _____

3. Do you celebrate Halloween or a holiday like it in your country? _____

_____

4. What is your birth date? _____

What is your horoscope sign? _____

What is associated with that sign? _____

Ask a partner to share answers to at least two of the above questions.

- *Extra Learning*

Direct and Indirect Quotations

Direct: Stevie called to say, "I still care about you."

Indirect: Stevie called to say how much he cares.

Can you compose direct and indirect quotations from the cues below? Use your imagination to fill in characters and quotes.

1. Linda Ronstadt / told[7] / her producer / *she wanted some coffee.* _____

   (direct) *Linda told her producer, "I want some coffee."* _____

   (indirect) *Linda told her producer that she wanted some coffee.* _____

2. Madonna / asked / costume designer / _____

   (direct) _____

   (indirect) _____

3. The businessman / asked / boss / _____

   (direct) _____

   (indirect) _____

4. The director of the company / told / _____ / _____

   (direct) _____

   (indirect) _____

told: past tense of **tell**

- ## *Hyphenated Adjectives*

The first box has a list of hyphenated adjectives. The second box has names of people and things. Mix and match from each box to compose your own story. You don't have to use every item, but see how many you can put into your story. Feel free to add your own adjectives, characters, and objects.

better-known	early-blooming	snow-capped
chocolate-covered	fine-sounding	well-dressed
delicious-tasting	good-looking	well-known

cake	man	Julio Iglesias
candy	mountain	John Lennon
child	woman	Luciano Pavarotti
flower	singer	Kyu Sakamoto

_____
_____
_____
_____
_____
_____
_____
_____

TRIVIA QUIZ

Make two teams. Take turns asking the questions below. The team with the most correct answers – without looking in the book– is the winner. If neither team knows an answer, then search for it in this Text/Workbook. There are two categories of questions. You may choose your category.

- ### ARTISTS AND PEOPLE

1. Who learned Mexican-American songs from her father? She also sings folk, rock, big-band and other styles of music. __ __ __ __ __   __ __ __ __ __ __ __ __

2. Who sang "What a Wonderful World"? His classmates called him "Satchel-Mouth" because of his big mouth. __ __ __ __ __   __ __ __ __ __ __ __ __ __ __

3. Who wrote and sang these words: "You may say I'm a dreamer"? __ __ __ __

   __ __ __ __ __ __

4. Who recorded his first big hit at age 13? He wrote "I Just Called to Say I Love You."

   __ __ __ __ __ __   __ __ __ __ __ __

5. Who was the daughter of a miner? She tripped and fell into the foaming brine.

   __ __ __ __ __ __ __ __ __ __ __

6. He is a blind pianist and singer. He is older than Stevie Wonder, and recorded the song "Georgia on My Mind" many years ago. Who is he? __ __ __   __ __ __ __ __ __ __ __

7. Who lived in Dublin, sold fish, and died of a fever? __ __ __ __ __

   __ __ __ __ __ __

8. Who was born in Russia, wrote many songs including "Anything You Can Do," and died at the age of 101? __ __ __ __ __ __   __ __ __ __ __ __

9. What is the name of the woman that the banjo-player travels to Louisiana to see? He tells her, "Don't you cry for me!" __ __ __ __ __ __ __

- ### CELEBRATIONS, DATES, PLACES, THINGS

1. What is the name of the holiday on December 25? Some people celebrate twelve days of gift giving beginning with this holiday. __ __ __ __ __ __ __ __ __

2. What was the year of the Gold Rush in California? __ __ __ __

3. What do we call a person who was in that Gold Rush?

   __ __ __ __ __ __ __   __ __ __ __ __ __

4. What are two kinds of shellfish that sweet Molly Malone sells?

   __ __ __ __ __ __ __ __ and __ __ __ __ __ __ __ __

5. What is the capital city of Ireland? __ __ __ __ __ __ __

6. Some say that the fruit of this tree is impossible to eat. Which tree is it?

   __ __ __ __ __ __ tree

7. Which holiday is celebrated on October 31, the day before All Saints' Day? Sometimes children dress up in costumes on this day. __ __ __ __ __ __ __ __ __

8. What is the name of the mountain where the woman lost her true love "from courting too slow"? __ __ __   __ __ __ __ __

9. In his song, what is the first thing that Stevie Wonder called to say?

   __   __ __ __ __   __ __ __

• *ASTROLOGICAL SIGNS*

Unscramble these horoscope signs, and choose the correct dates for each. See if you can find someone with a birthday to match each sign. Write in that person's name and exact birth date.

SIGN		DATES	PERSON + BIRTH DATE
srAie	_____	Mar. 21-Apr. 19	_____
surTua	_____	Apr. 20-May 20	_____
imineG	_____	May 21-June 20	_____
cnCaer	_____	June 21-July 22	_____
oLe	_____	July 23-Aug. 22	_____
orgVi	_____	Aug. 23-Sept. 22	_____
irLba	_____	Sept. 23-Oct. 22	_____
pooricS	_____	Oct. 23-Nov. 21	_____
suitStiaarg	_____	Nov. 22-Dec. 21	_____
ripaCcron	_____	Dec. 22-Jan. 19	_____
aqrsiuAu	_____	Jan. 20-Feb. 18	_____
sPceis	_____	Feb. 19-Mar. 20	_____

• DIRECT AND INDIRECT QUOTATIONS

Following is an imaginary conversation between Stevie Wonder and Madonna.

Stevie:	Hi, Madonna! What's up[1]?
Madonna:	Stevie, great to hear from you. Nothing much. Just got back from a concert tour in England.
Stevie:	How did it go?
Madonna:	Crowds were good, but I'm getting a little tired of wearing all those different clothes. How about you?
Stevie:	Well, I'm working on a new album with Rubén Blades and Quincy Jones. It's hot!
Madonna:	That's great. Listen, Stevie, I have to go. My makeup person is hollering at me. Sorry.
Stevie:	Yeah, I've got to get back to my keyboard. Talk to you later.

Practice reading the above conversation with a partner. Take turns being Stevie and Madonna. Now answer the following questions in two ways. The first time use direct quotes; the second time use indirect quotes.

1. What did Stevie say after he said "Hi" to Madonna?

   _____

   _____

2. What did Madonna say about her tour in England?

   _____

   _____

3. What did Stevie say he had to do?

   _____

   _____

• TELEPHONE CONVERSATIONS

Work with a partner to make up your own telephone conversations for the two following situations. Take turns playing the parts.

1. Call up a friend to ask if she/he wants to go to the movies with you a week from Saturday. Decide which movie, which theater, where you'll meet, when, etc.
2. Respond to the ad below.

[1] **What's up?:** an expression meaning "How are you doing?"

Irregular Verbs used in Level Three

VERB	PAST	PAST PARTICIPLE
be	was, were	been
become	became	become
begin	began	begun
buy	bought	bought
catch	caught	caught
come	came	come
dig	dug	dug
do	did	done
drive	drove	driven
eat	ate	eaten
fall	fell	fallen
feel	felt	felt
find	found	found
forget	forgot	forgotten
freeze	froze	frozen
get	got	gotten
give	gave	given
go	went	gone
have	had	had
hide	hid	hidden
keep	kept	kept
know	knew	known
leave	left	left
lie	lay	lain
lose	lost	lost
make	made	made

VERB	PAST	PAST PARTICIPLE
mean	meant	meant
rise	rose	risen
say	said	said
see	saw	seen
set	set	set
stand	stood	stood
take	took	taken
teach	taught	taught
tell	told	told
think	thought	thought
wear	wore	worn
win	won	won
withdraw	withdrew	withdrawn
write	wrote	written

ARTIST INDEX

Use this index to find a song by a particular composer, instrumental musician, or singer.

Use this index to find songs with a particular theme.

GENRE/THEME INDEX

Use this index to look up a particular grammatical usage or verb tense that you want to practice. We have included examples from the Introductions, the Songs, and from the Learning Ideas. When a song has many examples of a particular usage, we list one or two examples and add "+ others."

Abbreviation
CD = compact disc: "Frenesí" (Introduction), 77

Adjectives
Hyphenated: see Hyphenated Adjectives
Review: "What a Wonderful World," 20

Adverbs
Review: "Frenesí," 77; "Lemon Tree," 59
Superlative:
  It's most important: "Lemon Tree," 59

"As" + Clause
As she wheeled her wheelbarrow: "Cockles and Mussels," 40

"Can"
Anything you can do: "Anything You Can Do," 65

Clauses
When I first came + others: "When I First Came to This Land," 46
Review: "Clementine," 52
                                                                          "Frenesí," 77
                                                                          "Lemon Tree," 59
                                                                          "Oh, Susanna!," 72
                                                                          Review Two, 57

Comparative Adjectives
a sadder man but wiser now: "Lemon Tree," 59

Comparisons
worse than a thief, more lies than: "On Top of Old Smoky," 29
Review: "Anything You Can Do," 65
                                                                          "Frenesí," 77
                                                                          Review One, 27

"As" + Adjective + "As"
  corn is as high as: "Oh, What a Beautiful Mornin'," 8
  as sweet and clear as: "Georgia on My Mind," 14

"Like" + Noun
  cattle are standin' like statues: "Oh, What a Beautiful Mornin'," 8

"More than"
  learn much more than I'll ever know: "What a Wonderful World," 20

GRAMMATICAL INDEX

GRAMMATICAL INDEX

SONG INDEX

This index lists each of the fourteen songs in Level Three in alphabetical order.